# THE GUNCLE GUIDE

## TIPS, WISDOM, STORIES, AND ADVICE FOR EVERYONE'S FAVORITE FAMILY MEMBER

## GLENN GARNER

### PREFACE BY DANIEL FRANZESE
### FOREWORD BY JOHNNY SIBILLY

Skyhorse Publishing

Skyhorse Publishing books may be purchased in bulk at special discounts for sales promotion, corporate gifts, fund-raising, or educational purposes. Special editions can also be created to specifications. For details, contact the Special Sales Department, Skyhorse Publishing, 307 West 36th Street, 11th Floor, New York, NY 10018 or info@skyhorsepublishing.com.

Skyhorse® and Skyhorse Publishing® are registered trademarks of Skyhorse Publishing, Inc.®, a Delaware corporation.

Visit our website at www.skyhorsepublishing.com.

10 9 8 7 6 5 4 3 2 1

Library of Congress Cataloging-in-Publication Data

Names: Garner, Glenn, author.
Title: The guncle guide: a smart, stylish, funny guide for everyone's favorite family member / Glenn Garner; preface by Daniel Franzese; foreword by Johnny Sibilly.
Description: New York, NY: Skyhorse Publishing, [2020] |
Identifiers: LCCN 2020006204 (print) | LCCN 2020006205 (ebook) | ISBN 9781510757547 (hardcover) | ISBN 9781510757554 (ebook)
Subjects: LCSH: Uncles—Family relationships. | Gay men—Family relationships. | Nieces—Family relationships. | Nephews—Family relationships.
Classification: LCC HQ759.94 .G37 2020 (print) | LCC HQ759.94 (ebook) | DDC 306.85—dc23
LC record available at https://lccn.loc.gov/2020006204
LC ebook record available at https://lccn.loc.gov/2020006205

Cover design by Daniel Brount
Cover image from Getty Images

Print ISBN: 978-1-5107-5754-7
Ebook ISBN: 978-1-5107-5755-4

Printed in China

*To Mom, Dad, Christie, Mandy, Sarah Ann, Savanah, and Stephanie*

# Contents

# PREFACE

I would venture to say being a guncle is the greatest experience you can have with a kid. Being a parent is wonderful, but you are required to discipline and raise them 24/7. Grandparents have a good deal—they get to spoil the kids and give them back. But it's the guncle that still knows the current songs on the radio and the cool places to hang out. We get all the perks of grandparents and still get to be cool!

There is a special connection when you hold that infant in your arms. They can sense that you are family, and when they look into your eyes, there is an instant bond. They are born adoring you. As soon as they call you by name like "Unka Danny," those words will cut through even the coldest of hearts like a hot knife through butter.

We guncles are responsible for exposing our babies to culture and experiences their parents might not. So far, I have taught my nieces the art of thrift store shopping, where to get the perfect grilled cheese, and how to appreciate and love drag queens. We recently discovered L.O.L. Surprise! dolls' wigs fit on Ken. Barbie is shook!

I couldn't wait for my nieces to be old enough for me to take them to see musicals. I knew one of my major jobs as a guncle was to make sure they knew their Broadway. When my niece Italina was five, I took her to see *Gypsy*, and she just danced and enjoyed the show—but she was too young to remember it. Now she is the perfect age!

We sat over her new keyboard last Christmas, and I started to teach her "Tomorrow" from *Annie*. At first, she was resistant (she wanted to sing Ariana Grande and other pop princesses). She learned the songs, and then we sat to watch the movie. The next thing I knew, all of my

hard work as a guncle paid off. She knew every word to "Hard Knock Life," and she couldn't wait to see her next show. I have held onto this dream for years. It's finally time the prophecy is fulfilled!

This is where my role as guncle really comes in. I want to spoil my niece, this is true. Even more than that, I want her to have all the cultural benefits and childlike humor that we as queer people possess. I'll sit and put together her doll house and talk about every accessory. Just like Miss Hannagin, I've been blessed and surrounded by little girls. I have all my nieces: Italina, Kylie, Arianna, Olivia, and baby Emilia, and now my sister is pregnant with my first nephew Gerald. I'm so ready.

I don't know if God will one day put me in a position where I can adopt and become a parent but being a guncle is so close. I feel so happy and enriched with these loveable kids in my life. I love being a guncle.

Glenn is the perfect guncle to be writing the official book on the subject. Not only has he always shown kindness and patience, which are two of the keys to being a great guncle, but he also has twenty-two nieces and nephews. I thought I had my hands full. He's an expert, and I hope this book keeps you smiling and excited to spoil your little ones.

—**Daniel Franzese, Actor**
(***Mean Girls, Looking, Party Monster***)

# FOREWORD

I remember growing up and playing "aunt and uncle" with my little sister. We were so used to being taken care of by our own aunts and uncles when our parents would go out of town or just going to hang out with our cousins, that it felt like the perfect game. We'd drop off baby dolls and say, "I'll be back to pick them up!" "How'd she behave?" We'd ask each other about our fake children. Those times were the *best*.

I still remember where I was when my sister first told me she was pregnant. I remember immediately feeling a responsibility shift, being the big brother. I was beyond ready for the task. I remember telling everyone as if the baby were going to be my own. Growing up with my mom and sister as a trio, I absolutely felt closer and more responsible than I think most uncles would.

There was also that other thing: I was gay. All I ever knew of gay men was lives of loneliness and sickness from what I saw in the media. I never knew if I'd have my own kids, but I wanted nothing more than to be a dad. That's why it felt like a victory for me—even if I didn't have my own one day, I'd always have her, my beautiful niece Jasmine.

Being a guncle has been one of the greatest joys of my life. My niece shows me the world through a filter that isn't riddled with judgment and bitterness. She inspires me to be a kid again when I see her joy. I remember the first time we put on wigs together and shot a video for fun. It was our first real bonding experience where I felt totally myself.

I always joke that she's one of the reasons for my rise in followers on social media. The guncle video I did with her years ago got millions of views, and I think that's mostly because there is such a thirst for that relatable representation. So many queer people can relate to being that to their nieces and nephews, but the mainstream never really touches on it.

The joy and excitement she shows when she sees me will forever melt my heart. I'm so happy to live in a time where other gay men share their relationships with their families, so hopefully the world can learn to love queer folks more and realize that we can be wonderful

role models too. I'm blessed daily to have a sister that allows me to be a big part of my niece's growth into a wonderful young woman.

It made me so happy to read Glenn's book and know he's sharing his story and the story of so many of us too, that people don't usually get to see. He's worked incredibly hard in all other aspects of his life when it comes to his work at *OUT Magazine*, etc., and it's nice to see a personal side being shown that so many of us can relate to. When we guncles stick together, we can move mountains with joy and love. Glenn has both of those and more!

**—Johnny Sibilly, Actor**
**(*Pose, The Deuce, Liza on Demand*)**

# INTRODUCTION

Everyone has that one family member who they're genuinely most excited to see over the holidays or at family functions. It might not always be appropriate to admit it, but lesbi-honest: we all have a favorite. It's usually the cool older cousin or the wise-cracking aunt.

If you find yourself fortunate enough, it's likely the guncle (gay uncle, if you're not up to date with your millennial slang and hashtags). The guncle is one of the most widely beloved yet undersung family members of the 21$^{st}$ century. But we've managed to win over many in recent years, as inclusion for the LGBTQ community becomes more prevalent.

Yes, guncles have been around as long as gay men (so as long as the human race), whether out and proud among their families or forced to refer to their serious partners as their roommates. You might have only learned about them through faint whispers at the dinner table not intended for your impressionable adolescent ears, or perhaps you've seen them in your favorite movie or sitcom, or maybe in adorable photos on your Instagram feed. Still, we've always been here. Famous guncles in history you might have heard of include (but are definitely not limited to) Oscar Wilde, James Baldwin, Tab Hunter, RuPaul Charles, and Andy Cohen.

With the 21st century, the guncle has become a more widely accepted familial staple. Thanks to social media, he's celebrated *en masse*, a serious contender with cat memes and videos of soldiers reuniting with their dogs. And given the growing representation in film and television, we're seeing ourselves on the screen more and more often.

In recent years, we've even acquired our own holiday (the second Sunday in August, in case you need time to find the perfect gift). Royal baby Archie also has his own unofficial guncle in mommy Meghan Markle's makeup artist and close friend Daniel  Martin. We've risen from the cheap punchline and piece of shameless gossip to a (dare I say it) respected and adored part of any family lucky enough to have us.

# Chapter 1

# THE YOUNG GUNCLE

As a proud guncle of twenty-two nieces and nephews (yes, I'm serious), I've gained years of experience and memorable moments. With the old school and often tone-deaf nature of our baby boomer predecessors and the empowering and inclusive spirits of Generation Z, it's often the guncle who bridges the gap, providing a unique perspective to most family dynamics. It's a role that comes with responsibility—it's not often easy, but the serious moments are usually rivaled by the joyful experiences.

Before I get into the anecdotes and tidbits of wisdom, it feels necessary to share a glimpse at my family tree. It's rooted in my hometown of Jackson, Mississippi, and it branches as far as Washington State and Greece, so bear with me.

I don't remember the exact order of events. I was only three years old, after all. But there are several details that stand out . . .

My dad held me up to the hospital window where the newborns were on display for doting family members. There were only two babies in there, one black and one white. He asked if I could guess which one was my niece, a question that genuinely left me perplexed, as my innocent naivety had not yet been scathed by the many social flaws of our world. I looked up at him and asked, "Both?"

When he clarified that it was in fact the baby with milky white skin and blonde hair (almost as milky white), I was suddenly distracted by her round red pacifier, which almost looked like a nose. That inspired my follow-up question, "Is she a clown?"

My first niece, Cassie, was born in late 1994. Her mom, my half-sister Joan from my mom's side, went into labor around midnight. She gave birth to her firstborn at exactly noon that day. I didn't join them at the hospital until around 4:00 in the afternoon.

Joan turned out to be a great mom, not to mention a great sister and one of the most supportive figures in my life. With another three kids in her future and a strong marriage, she ultimately became my first real-life example of what a "normal" family looks like, as my own parents had divorced by the time I hit puberty.

With the addition of Cassie, as well as Joan's husband-to-be, Luke, we were the same happy family, plus two. And although I might have been subconsciously jealous of the attention my first niece was receiving (perhaps not so subconsciously, given the tantrums preserved in time on my mom's home video collection), I was still fiercely protective of this little girl.

Joan's firstborn was also the first time I witnessed a pregnancy and the beginning of a new human life. While I was still wildly too young for "the talk," I knew there was a baby growing in my sister's belly, and I was fascinated. The fascination increased tenfold when Cassie was actually born.

Given our miniscule age difference, we were soon attending the same preschool, where I showed her off to my friends like she was the Game Boy I swiped from my sister Devyn and tried to pass as my own. As the baby of my family who desperately wanted a younger sibling, I never quite expected her to be the addition to fill that gap.

Although not even old enough to tie my shoes or properly pronounce the word "library," I took my role as an uncle very seriously. My grandfather, who was always a joyful and humorous spirit, convinced me one day that he was going to leave and take Cassie with him.

*Children have never been very good at listening to their elders, but they have never failed to imitate them.*

—James Baldwin
(writer, activist, guncle)

So, I did the only logical thing that made sense and locked him out of the house. A month later, my half-brother Ollie from my dad's side was in town for a rare visit. He offered me a swing set in exchange for Cassie, an agreement I'm not proud to say I accepted. It just goes to show that everyone has their price.

Not long after, Joan and Luke moved away with Cassie, bouncing around from one naval base to the next until ultimately settling down in South Carolina. Along the way, they accumulated two more daughters, Dakota and Beck, and a son, Nico.

The next sibling to bite the bullet was my sister Vada, my oldest sibling and only half-sister from my dad's side. Her wedding (also to a navy man) was one of the few occasions I saw her in my lifetime, which became more and more sporadic as I got older—a result of her strained relationship with our dad, which subsequently rippled down to her relationship with me.

They also bounced around as a military family, bringing my nephews Miles and Trey and my niece Birdie into the world. I've only seen them a handful of times in their lives, and I could swear that they're different people each time, every visit separated by multiple years and significant life events. Birdie manages to keep the same joyful spirits every time she sees me, while the other two are well into their teens with their own lives taking shape.

By the time I was in high school, my mom had married her fourth husband, Eddie, after several years of dating and successful cohabitating. With her new hubby came three new stepsisters: Bryce, Lina, and Tatum.

Bryce was already set in the motherhood department, with toddler triplets of her own, daughters Jaime and Rikki and son Reese. I've witnessed them shoot up to the tall gangly teens they are today from the adorable toddlers they were when I first met them, not to mention all the awkward years in between.

Tatum was also already a mom to a baby boy of her own, a joyfully energetic little spirit named Leo. He was followed by three girls: Stella, Violet, and Mia. But since they live in Chicago, our visits are too few and far in between.

Lina soon gave birth to her first as well, a son named Asher. I babysat him on a few occasions, and I was a total hit with my expert Elmo impression. I fell asleep once while I was supposed to be watching him, and he took off down our cul-de-sac, having recently learned to walk and operate doorknobs (don't worry, he barely made it past the driveway before my mom caught him). When he was a little older, I woke up to a swift slap in the face from Asher after I fell asleep on the couch, so I consider us even.

A few years later, Lina welcomed Carson, who was Asher's identical mini with an adorably tiny pair of eyeglasses as a toddler. Family members frequently compared him to the little boy from *Jerry Maguire*.

My brother Ollie, my only brother in a sea of sisters, didn't have his first kid until his second marriage. His first was actually his first and second, as he fathered twin boys Gavin and Gabe, blond spitting images of photos I've seen of my brother as a kid. The twins were followed by beautiful baby girl Nina, a New Year's baby.

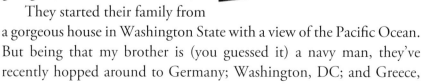

I didn't see much of Ollie growing up, but the few visits we did share would become some of my fondest childhood memories. I'd always hoped he would become a father, as he inherited an unmistakably warm paternal nature from our dad. I honestly felt left out that he and his wife Chloe told our dad they were pregnant first, and I had to find out with the rest of the world, but I don't hold grudges (at least not in this case).

They started their family from a gorgeous house in Washington State with a view of the Pacific Ocean. But being that my brother is (you guessed it) a navy man, they've recently hopped around to Germany; Washington, DC; and Greece,

providing their kids with some rich culture and early life experiences I often envy.

Devyn, my second oldest half-sister from my mom's side, held out for a while. I recall one awkward occasion when our mom and our neighbor tried to set her up with an apparently nice young man, randomly inviting him over once when she was drying off from taking a dip in our inflatable pool. She eventually became stepmother to Brandon and Neil when she got married to Matt. They later gave me my final nephew (so far), Kirby, a few days before I came home after graduating from Northern Arizona University. Although still an infant at the time, he became my best friend in those uncomfortable but formative post-college years.

In case you've lost count (don't worry, I often forget some of their names), that's three half-sisters, one half-brother, and three stepsisters, resulting in a whopping *twenty-two* nieces and nephews spread around the United States and Europe. What can I say? I'm from the south.

I've always loved being part of a big family. Holidays at my grandmother's house were rarely boring with a tribe of children always running around. But over the years, it's often been hard not to feel alone in such a brood. No matter how accepting your family is, that's an easy feeling to exhibit as a queer person—knowing that the people closest to you can't fully understand what you go through, no matter how hard they try.

## Guncle Wisdom

Belonging to a large family doesn't necessarily mean having a large support system. As a queer person, it's often easy to feel alone when nobody you know seems to understand or accept you. And we're one of the rare minorities that are saddled from an early age with the fear that our families will disown us for our identity. A study conducted by Chapin Hall at the University of Chicago found that LGBTQ youth were 120% more likely to experience homelessness than their cisgender heterosexual counterparts.

If it feels like there's no one to talk to, The Trevor Project is an indispensable resource for LGBTQ youth. Their confidential toll-free lifeline is open 24/7, offering a safe and judgment-free space for times of crisis. They can be reached at 1-866-488-7386 or online at TheTrevorProject.org.

## *Takeaways*

- With 22 nieces and nephews, I've gained a lifetime of knowledge on gunclehood.
- Even with a big family, it's easy to feel alone as a queer person.

# Chapter 2

# A GUNCLE IS BORN

Technically, I've been a guncle for most of my life. But I didn't quite claim the label for the first seventeen years. That would require claiming the label of a gay man, which is rarely an easy process.

I say "process," because that's what it was for me—and is for so many in the LGBTQ community. I didn't come out to the world in one big grand gesture with a viral YouTube video. My coming out came shortly before the It Gets Better era, which seemed to open the floodgates of social media inclusion, equipping Gen-Z with the empowerment they continue to fearlessly display.

But even for those queer influencers who seem to live their lives truthfully and courageously, I assure you their coming out was a process, too.

Simon Dunn, a rugby player and former Australian Olympic hopeful in bobsledding, revealed how he started his process: "My

niece was actually the first person I ever told. She was a baby, and her being a twin, I'd help my sister with feeding. It was before I'd come out and didn't have the confidence to tell anyone in my family. I guess at the time, it was nice to be able to say it out loud to someone."

I guess you could say the five stages of grieving apply in the process of coming out (at least for me). Although instead of grieving the loss of another life, it's the life you thought you had or needed: the perceived normalcy of a heteronormative future.

The denial is an obvious one, as no boy growing up in Jackson, Mississippi, during the '90s wants to admit they're the thing that everyone talks about in such a demeaning manner. Anger came with the middle school bullies who gave me my own sense of self-hatred. As for bargaining, I figured I'd get it out of my system when I was young, maybe have one downlow experience before committing to a life in a straight monogamous relationship. And depression is too often a dangerous, but unfortunately common, thing for queer kids. But for me, it's what fueled the acceptance, because I knew I'd never be happy if I didn't live my life honestly.

The process doesn't end there though, as having a strong support system is just as important as developing your own sense of self-acceptance. My friend Nick Fager, a psychotherapist and founder of Expansive Therapy who specializes in LGBTQ clients, as well as

*I am totally fearless! Well, of course, I'm not totally fearless. I worry constantly and obsess over things, but I just don't let fear stand in the way of doing something that I really want to do.*

—Tom Ford (fashion designer, filmmaker, guncle)

the mind behind the popular queer mental health-driven Instagram @gaytherapy, explains why.

He says, "Coming out to a hostile environment, though very common and often brushed over as 'normal' to some extent, is an extremely traumatic event. For most of us, that is the most vulnerable moment of our lives up until that point, and when it is met with hostility, it reinforces the defenses that we have already spent so long erecting and puts us into an increased state of post-traumatic hypervigilance.

"This is why it is so important to have at least one person who affirms us for exactly who we are. That one person can give us the courage we need to emerge into the world, not just as gay or queer people, but as our entire unique selves. If you haven't found that person, you need to make it your primary mission, because no growth or healing happens before we find safety."

As important as I knew it was, the thought of coming out to my family all together was infinitely more daunting than squaring off against any middle school bully. I thought it best to take it one person at a time, but for some reason, it felt easier to be truthful with a stranger at first.

That's why the first person I told was Scott, a freshman football player at Mississippi College, a notoriously Christian institution. We met on MySpace in the final weeks of my senior year of high school. Our online exchange was followed by an awkward rendezvous at his older ex-boyfriend's apartment, where he frequently stayed to avoid the dorms.

A week later, I came out to my best friend Blue while driving around Flowood in the middle of the night. He was the only openly gay person I knew, so telling him felt like the natural next step. Blue became my rock that summer as I jumped headfirst into the local gay scene. He's since come out as a Trump supporter, so we don't talk anymore.

The first family member I decided to have the conversation with was my sister Devyn. She was the closest in age, and she'd recently become my closest sibling after years of playing the annoyed-older-sister and pesky-younger-brother dynamic.

I use the term "conversation" loosely though, as there was little talking involved. I had it all planned out, making a reservation for us at Biaggi's, my favorite Italian restaurant in Ridgeland. Every time I thought the words would escape my mouth, the waiter came back to check on us. By the time the tiramisu had come, I still wasn't able to muster the courage or even articulate what I desperately needed to voice.

Instead, I texted her from across the table, perhaps partially in fear that someone at the next table would overhear (even though I'd already mastered coming out to strangers on the Internet). Although it wasn't a totally uplifting afterschool special moment, it still went about as well as I could have hoped. She responded with love, but not exactly with understanding—that would come later, as it did with most of my family.

I came out to my dad next, and this time, I was actually able to verbalize it. It didn't go quite as well, though. The conversation took place while we assembled a grill, which we'd bought earlier that day from Home Depot. I can't fully remember the events, but either I cried, he cried, or maybe we both cried.

He feared that not having a wife or a conventional lifestyle in my future would mean I couldn't be happy. But he eventually came to realize what I realized, that coming out was the only way I *could* be happy.

With my mom, it wasn't so much of a coming out moment as it was an ambush. She confronted me during a commercial break while we binged a *One Tree Hill* marathon one afternoon. It came after two days of her stewing in the details of my diary, which she found while putting my laundry on my bed.

It was a brand-new diary but one of the first entries was about my first kiss with a boy. His name was Dylan, another guy I met on MySpace, before driving to visit him in Mobile on the weekend of my eighteenth birthday. We kept driving to Pensacola, where we stayed the night in a Red Roof Inn after going to see *I Love You, Beth Cooper*. Thank goddess it remained a PG night, or else my mom would have had a much more interesting read.

After the initial shock and betrayal of my mom reading my diary, the conversation calmed down. It went better than I would have expected, even though I was ultimately robbed of my own coming out.

But luckily, I had fair warning, as my mom called Devyn after reading, who called Joan. Joan tipped me off, but that also meant I wasn't able to come out to her on my own terms. She and I still had a

## Guncle Wisdom

Coming out to your family is like Black Friday shopping—it's best done through a strategic series of attacks. Unless you come from an uber-accepting 21st-century family of liberal hippies and you're positive they'll take the news well, it's best not to go with a grand gesture coming out moment.

Make your way through the family tree as you see fit. Pick who you think is the most accepting family member first and have a conversation with them in a safe space. If all goes well and they respond with nothing but positivity, you have an instant ally and a supporter as you make your way through telling the rest of your family.

chance to talk about it later that month, between chapters of the *Wicked* audiobook while I drove her to a doctor's appointment in Charlotte. I think by that time, I'd found my groove, as there was no tension in the moment, only a feeling of content. It helped that she knew exactly what to say, one of the most evolved in my family.

Coming out to Ollie was a moment I'm not too proud of, almost as graceful as my mom's ambush. It's possible that being out to most of my family had made me a little cocky and overly nonchalant when it came to breaking the news to everyone else.

It felt empowering to not care what people thought for possibly the first time in my life, cutting the homophobes out of my life with the rest of the people from high school I didn't intend to stay in touch with. But for a brief not-so-shining moment, I forgot that blood is thicker than adolescent ties.

During a phone call to catch up on my life, Ollie asked if I'd been dating anyone. I told him about the cheerleader I made out with the night before, careful not to mention names or gender pronouns. He asked me to text a photo, so I sent one of Shane, the University of Central Florida student with rock-hard abs who was a featured extra in *Bring It On: In It to Win It*.

Ollie responded in appropriate confusion, slightly angry that I sprang the news on him with such little care. He didn't talk to me for a week, which I wasn't as bothered by, because we rarely spoke. Still consumed in my overconfidence, I didn't grasp that he needed space.

When he did get back to me, he was in a much better place about the situation. His then-girlfriend Chloe, who I hadn't met yet, helped him realize that his issues with my sexuality were just that, his own. Now his wife, she still holds a special place in my heart because of that moment.

It wasn't until Ollie and Chloe's wedding that I finally told Vada. Although that was more because she asked me in a matter-of-fact manner after seeing numerous photos of me with drag queens at the local 18-and-up gay club Dick & Jane's. She seemed unbothered by the revelation but happy to find out.

With my stepsisters, there was never a pressure to come out to them. They were grown and leading their own families by the time our parents met, and I was a teenager with my own self-instilled sense of seclusion. As they're also devout Pentecostals, there never felt like a good enough reason to tell them myself.

I was forced into going to their church one Sunday, which turned out to be an intense experience of old white people chanting

in tongues and running up and down the aisles as the Holy Spirit ran through them. It was more than Megan Fox could ever prepare me for. Although, it was the same church where Sacha Baron Cohen got baptized in *Borat* (not that the preacher likes to discuss it), so that was cool. But given our family's southern sense of well-intentioned idle gossip, my stepsisters likely learned about my identity through a secondhand source.

RJ Kennedy, a family lawyer in Jacksonville, Florida, seems to have had a similar coming out process as I had with most of my family. He told me, "My coming out process, as difficult as it was for me, was made so much easier because of the reaction I received from my siblings and their partners."

He also adds a helpful tip for broaching the topic with younger family members: "When it comes to the kids, every once in a while, for a holiday or birthday, I'll find just the right children's book to introduce a message that love has no gender, but I'll always give their parents a heads up."

Amid this series of often intense family moments, I never had the chance to tell my nieces or nephews personally. I never felt comfortable telling them, to be honest. Being raised in the south, the idea of "What should I tell my kids?" was constantly nailed into my head as a justification for homophobia, as if the existence of diversity was somehow a detriment to society.

But it still felt important for them to know, some way or another. Fager says, "Our family members aren't just people in our lives. They are voices in our heads, and they play a role in our inner world. They become introjected into our psyche over time, and this is the case for any family member or close relationship who we spend a lot of time with. So, if you aren't out to certain generations, that is a part of yourself which you can't really integrate fully." He adds, "That takes a toll, if only subconsciously. Coming out to different generations of family, as well as our friends and networks, allows us to integrate internally."

Ultimately, I left it to my siblings to have that talk the way they saw fit. Over the years, as I've grown more comfortable in my skin, the stigma has somewhat lifted away. With most of my nieces and nephews, I either know or can safely assume by now that they've been informed.

Devyn recently assured me that she and Matt had that talk with their boys when they thought it was the right time. Regardless of my skepticism, my siblings have never really let me down when it came to representing me in an honest and loving way to their kids.

Joan once told me that Cassie was on to me from an early age. Whenever we'd visit, I always ended up playing with her Barbies, trying to convince her it was her idea. If it wasn't that, it was screening her vast collection of Mary-Kate and Ashley movies.

Cassie brought it up one day when they were driving around. Joan had told her that it was just that I thought the Olsen twins were pretty. But my niece wasn't quite sold on that excuse, telling her mom, "No, I don't think that's it." One thing I've always been confident in is Joan's maternal instinct for raising her kids with a sense of love and acceptance for others. Once they knew, there was never any judgment. In fact, they were more interested to hear about my life, genuinely curious about my otherness.

It was actually a pleasant surprise, the reactions from my nieces and nephews. But I guess it shouldn't be such a shock, as they belong to a much more inclusive generation. They mostly grew up without the sense of ignorance instilled in my peers from an early age.

It was a similar experience for Francesco "Franco" De Marco, whom I met through my favorite New York drag queen Ari Kiki at a classic New York pastime, drag brunch. But as a gay man who's also trans, there was twice the pressure. "The trans conversation has come up in the past with the oldest. I'm sure we'll re-broach it when they get older. They have met my husband and past boyfriends. My nephew just made his family tree and wrote Uncle Franco and my husband as Uncle Jean."

He continued, "Children are relatively innocuous, really. They just know the person as they grow and develop personality. Them being exposed to new and unique kinds of people becomes a norm. To them, it's no different than his dad's sisters and his dad's sister's husband."

## Takeaways

- Coming out is typically best done as a process, not a grand gesture.
- Finding even one ally in your family can help the process go more smoothly.
- Respect your siblings' wishes when coming out to their children

## Guncle Wisdom

If you have an openly queer sibling, relative, or close friend, your child deserves to know that. It could save their life one day.

A study by the Center for Disease Control and Prevention found that lesbian, gay, and bisexual youth seriously contemplate suicide at almost three times the rate of their heterosexual counterparts. They're also almost five times as likely to have attempted suicide.

Knowing just one LGBTQ person can change that. According to The Trevor Project's National Survey on LGBTQ Youth Mental Health, queer kids who had at least one accepting adult in their lives were 40 percent less likely to report a suicide attempt. More than one quarter of those who did not have an accepting adult did report attempting suicide, compared to 17 percent of those with a supportive figure.

# Chapter 3

· · · · · · · · · · · · · · · · · · · · · · · · · · · ·

# THE SILENCE
# OF THE GUNCLE

**W**orking up the courage to tell my family was a big deal. And luckily, it wasn't a tragic scene from some Oscar-bait flick that ends in either a hate crime or an AIDS-related death. But they didn't suddenly join their local chapters of PFLAG or march with me in Pride parades, either. If you're fortunate enough to avoid the worst of Mississippi's ignorance, you might find a more passive, less confrontational form of opposition.

My nieces and nephews have often been the only exception. The obvious and most logical reasoning is that they belong to a much more progressive generation. When I feel ignored or silenced by the majority of my family, it's the youngest ones who make me feel seen. Sure, it sometimes feels like I'm perpetually seated at the kids' table, but as a queer person, I've learned not to take inclusivity for granted.

Even after I'd laid my cards on the table, there was a bit of a Don't Ask, Don't Tell policy implemented among my family. My dad's side was pretty warm and open in regard to asking about my life. But my mom's side was a bit more traditional. And her husband Eddie's family (whom we'd come to spend most holidays with) was prominently religious Pentecostals.

Since moving to Los Angeles and developing my appreciation for cannabis, I've admittedly enjoyed a puff or two of Indica at recent family gatherings to calm my nerves. Sure, it helps build a hearty appetite for my stepdad's deep-fried turkey and my aunt's macaroni and cheese. It's also sometimes necessary when I feel obligated to stay silent about my life, as well as bite my tongue when they say something ignorant.

One shining example was when they bought a Google Home, which they apparently thought worked like a magic eight-ball, asking questions like, "Okay Google, is Hillary Clinton guilty?"

After heading off to college in Arizona, I'd turned over a new, more empowered leaf with my path to self-discovery. I'd even been elected to social chair for my college's gay/straight alliance, People Respecting Individuals and Sexual Minorities (PRISM . . . like a rainbow, get it?).

But not everyone was as overwhelmed with joy as I was about my newfound self-awareness. My first semester was coming to a close, and I was preparing to head home to Jackson for the month-long winter break. During a call with my mom, she had one request for my visit: "Just don't talk about sex or anything."

I was frankly baffled that this was somehow a concern, as if I had ever been the kind of person comfortable discussing sex around my family; goddess knows none of my straight siblings brought up those kinds of topics at Thanksgiving dinner. And this request was coming from the woman who supported our family as a Passion Parties consultant for most of my life, a now-shuttered company that was marketed toward couples trying to reignite the spark in their relationship. It was difficult to explain to my peers when I was a kid, but I never judged her for it and always respected her work ethic as a single mom.

There's an unfortunate stigma associated with sexuality, the same sense of shame we feel growing up, thinking we can't ask the crucial questions that are so often avoided by the abstinence-only convictions of public schools and church-driven communities. But as queer people, we quickly learn after coming out that being queer is not all about sex. While we try to feel empowered in that subculture of our community, given the shame and oppression we've been forced to feel about it for most of our lives, our history and culture is much richer and more vibrant than topics of cruising and bathhouse orgies (which is perfectly fine conversation in the right company).

My mom can always tell when she's said the wrong thing or made her children feel bad, and she makes an effort to learn from her mistakes. She didn't suddenly plant a rainbow flag in the front yard, but she did put a deck of nude male playing cards in my stocking that year for me to open on Christmas Eve after the nieces and nephews went to bed. It was a silly novelty gift that made me laugh, but it also gave me an unexpected sense of familial validation I didn't realize I needed.

Things didn't suddenly change for the better with my mom, as we don't openly communicate about every aspect of my life. She's rarely even asked about my love life (granted, one of the only boyfriends of mine that she met dumped me the next day). She didn't even seem to take much of an interest in my career when I worked at the largest circulated LGBTQ publication in the country. Although she rarely brought it up with me personally, Joan would assure me that mom always brought it up in their private conversations, printing off my articles or raving about my accomplishments and how proud she was of me. I guess it's not always easy to tell people directly how you really feel, especially in my family.

Luckily, my nieces haven't been as shy about taking that kind of interest in my life. They're always the ones asking if I have a boyfriend or if I ever plan on getting married. One of my older nieces even offered up her surrogacy services, something I took with gratitude, but also a grain of salt as she was blinded by the novelty of gay dads and hadn't even learned to take care of herself yet (not that I had mastered that skill either). I never quite had the heart to break it to them that gay relationships are often more complex than their enduring high school sweetheart romances, and that although we've finally

## Guncle Wisdom

Finding that one safe family member can help to gauge where the rest of them stand. They can also be the life raft that gets you through the often-uncomfortable family gatherings, where you might feel silenced.

If that person doesn't exist in your family, find a good friend and let them know you might need some emotional support. When triggering moments arrive at home, send your friend a text to vent or just to keep your mind occupied. If possible, invite them to your family gathering, as a social buffer is always a good idea.

won the right to get married, we don't jump into monogamy quite as quickly or recklessly as our straight counterparts.

I haven't been able to have these talks with all my nieces and nephews, but it's not for a lack of trying (on my part or theirs). Just as it is with coming out to nieces and nephews, it's always necessary to defer to their parents with these kinds of talks, regardless of what you feel is appropriate.

During one family vacation, my nephews Brandon and Neil were drilling me with questions while out at dinner. It was mostly about if I had any games on my phone, before one of them asked, "Do you have a girlfriend?" My sister Devyn snapped at them to shut up. I'm sure it was partially due to the stress of the day, but I could also tell she wasn't ready for them to have that discussion.

Something similar happened with Joan. She's always been nothing but supportive, but being that Nico is her youngest and the only boy, she's slightly more protective of him. Given that he's approaching a formative age, I respected her wishes but also reminded her that I was his age around the time I started discovering myself, and knowing I had a queer person in my family would have made all the difference. He's fortunate enough to have a gay friend, but the often-cruel politics of middle school (especially in South Carolina) can still make those social dynamics difficult to navigate.

Then there was also an unfortunate moment with Vada a few years ago that left me gobsmacked, to say the least. It seemed to come out of nowhere as I'd felt nothing but support from her during that trip, one of the few times I'd seen her in my life.

It was January of 2017, and I was staying with her before she drove me to the first Women's March on Washington, which I covered for *OUT Magazine*. We struck up conversation after she picked me up from the bus

*If you can't love yourself, how in the hell are you gonna love somebody else? Can I get an amen?*

—RuPaul Charles
(drag icon, guncle)

station, revealing that she and her husband had butted heads as he voted for Trump and she was a Hillary supporter. I updated her on my life and the things I was writing for work, including a phone interview with a queer literary icon I took in the privacy of her guest bedroom. As she dropped me back at the bus station at the end of the trip, I brought up some silly fact about *RuPaul's Drag Race*, which I'd been covering extensively. After acting cagey for the past couple of days, she finally said, "I just don't understand why it has to be shoved in everyone's faces."

It comes back to the crucial distinction that LGBTQ culture is not all about sex, an argument I couldn't quite form as we were approaching my destination. I didn't know what to say, so I just said nothing.

It also comes back to the tired argument that's become nothing more than an over-rehearsed conservative talking point in attempt to justify homophobia: "What am I supposed to tell my kids?" It's as if explaining that two men (or two women) can love each other is somehow a more difficult conversation than instructing kids on what to do in the very serious likelihood of a school shooting.

The truth is that children are never too young to learn that people different from them exist and deserve respect, and those conversations almost never have to include talk of sex. Adults often underestimate their kids' capacity for information, kids that are frequently bombarded with frightening facts and images in everyday life.

Regardless, it's always important to have those conversations with their parents before opening up with your nieces and nephews. You can try to nail a sense of wokeness and social responsibility into your siblings' heads as much as you want, but it's not your place to overstep their parenting. All you can do is be there and be ready to jump in when the time is right.

## Guncle Wisdom

Choose your battles. It's sometimes necessary to test (but not push) your boundaries when it comes to educating your family, but always proceed with caution.

On that note, public declarations in group situations are rarely as good an idea as one-on-one conversations in personal settings that make them feel less threatened. Approach the important topics with a calm sense of understanding, as opposed to a confrontational attitude. It's not easy admitting you're wrong when you feel attacked by the other person.

## Takeaways

- Establish boundaries for what's considered appropriate conversation with your family.
- As their thinking progresses over time, don't be afraid to test those boundaries every now and then.
- Usually belonging to a more progressive generation, nieces and nephews can often provide a safe space that other family members may not.

# THE GUNCLE BUCKET LIST

As a guncle, the most important gift you can give to your nieces and nephews is your time. It's the moments you make that they'll remember the most. And for every stage of their life, there are plenty of important experiences to be made, be they fun or educational (or ideally a combination of the two).

With straight family members, you'll often get uncles who take you hunting or mud-riding, aunts who opt for pageants and makeovers. Granted, those might be extreme examples (and proof that you can take the gay boy out of the south, but you can't take the cynicism out of the gay boy), but you get the idea. There's usually a sense of gender stereotypes attached to the kind of heteronormative bonding most grow up with, whether intentional or not.

But with a guncle, there's less pressure to live up to a societal standard or some need to conform to gender roles. We've grown up with plenty of other people's views imposed on us, so we make an effort not to treat others that way. Plus, we know some creative ways to make the most of a Sunday afternoon.

I've been fortunate enough to have some memorable moments with my nieces and nephews over the years. Although we don't always get the chance to break away from the rest of the family during our increasingly sporadic visits, we try to make the most of it when we

do. And to help spark some creative ideas for bonding moments, I've developed a bucket list of sorts.

Admittedly I haven't checked off everything on my own guncle bucket list (gunket list?), and there's a chance I won't be able to. But I try to put my best foot forward as a guncle, making myself available for as many of the big life moments as possible, and that's often all you can do.

## Ages 1–11

### ☐ Teach them our history

The reason ignorance is so prevalent in this country is because there's an overwhelming unwillingness to learn, a stubborn quality that gets worse over time. If you try to instill a sense of awareness and understanding for other cultures from a young age, perhaps you can help curb that societal error.

You can do so by teaching them the fundamentals of queer history. From the Stonewall riots of 1969 to the AIDS crisis of the '80s and everything in between, there's a never-ending well of culture to pull from. And although there are strides being made, they won't have another chance to learn these things until schools start adapting more honest and diverse lesson plans.

## ☐ Play dress up

Dress up is one of those childhood rites of passage that contributes to who we become as a person. Since most of our parents pick out our clothes until we're old enough to put our foot down, it's usually the first opportunity for creative self-expression through fashion. It's also an outlet for gender exploration that children in our society are all too often deprived of.

I played plenty of dress up in my day, and there's even video evidence of my sisters putting me in a wig and makeup when I was barely two years old. With only three years difference between us, I was still exploring my fashion sense by the time Cassie started exploring hers, which made for some great early bonding moments. But don't forget—you're never too old for dress up.

## ☐ Take them to a Pride parade

As much as alt-right propaganda might lead you to believe, Pride is not about sex, but a celebration of life. It has been since the first New York City Pride March in 1970, a year after our ancestors decided to fight back at Stonewall Inn and live their lives fully and truthfully. Although it's become more of a corporate-sponsored parade over the years, the spirit is still there and stronger than ever.

Every child should have the opportunity to attend a Pride parade or one of the many family Pride events available in most big cities. Growing up with straight conservative parents in heteronormative small-town America doesn't always present that opportunity, which is where a guncle comes in. It will be a fun time for everyone, as well as a moment of cultural enlightenment and education.

☐ **Introduce them to Joan Jett or [insert favorite queer icon]**

Joan Jett is a trailblazer among women in rock, as well as a musical icon whose work transcends generations. Although her sexual identity has always been a bit ambiguous, she's remained an undersung queer icon over the years. Her songs have been the soundtrack to some of my most pivotal moments in life, from the down and dark to the good and the uplifting.

From Lady Gaga to David Bowie, there's at least one queer musical icon for everyone to connect to. Find the one that you resonate with and share them with those who mean the most to you, particularly your nieces and nephews. Better yet, encourage them to find their own musical icon who can provide a soundtrack for their lives.

## Ages 12–20

☐ **Take them to their first concert**

When you're separated by hundreds of miles and only get to see each other once or twice a year, it's these big life moments that make a difference. Going to your first concert is that rite of passage when your mere fandom transcends into a fully realized cultural experience. And if your first is someone like Lizzo or Lady Gaga, it can also be an overwhelming moment of empowerment.

I've unfortunately yet to have this experience with my own nieces and nephews. But I was lucky enough to share my first concert with my older brother Ollie during one of our rare visits when I was 13 years old, and I flew to see him in Virginia Beach. It was Sara Bareilles opening for Maroon 5, and while neither are particularly iconic, it was a seminal moment in an overall happy adolescence.

## ☐ Take them to a big city

Growing up in middle America can be limiting for those with wild imaginations. It's important for everyone to experience the opportunities and possibilities available outside their hometown—begin with any larger city you can access, and over time you can work your way up to such cultural meccas as New York City and Los Angeles!

I was fortunate enough to be my niece Cassie's tour guide in New York after she graduated high school. Although a car or a new MacBook are always good choices for a grad gift, it was a chance to broaden her horizons which she truly appreciated. We even visited her first gay bar during our trip.

## ☐ Take them to a Broadway show

Every child has that one musical they sing nonstop for at least three months (okay, maybe not *every* child, but definitely the best ones). For me, there were two. With the short-lived Broadway musical adaptation of the Olivia Newton-John cult classic *Xanadu*, it was mostly because I had a massive pubescent crush on Cheyenne Jackson. With the more impactful *Spring Awakening*, I connected to the very real heartbreaking teen angst . . . and I also had a massive crush on Jonathan Groff.

My friend Anthony took me to my first Broadway musical, *Priscilla, Queen of the Desert,* during one of my summer internships. As a former theater nerd myself, I recognized the familiar rush of seeing a live performance, which was magnified tenfold by a Broadway caliber production. It reignited a childlike sense of wonder, which children of every age should experience at least once in their lives. (A live television event does not count.)

## ☐ Have a queer movie marathon

There are so many queer and queer-friendly cinematic examples of excellence (some of which I'll touch on a little later). From the historical significance of *Milk* to the unabashed camp of *Hairspray* (the John Waters-directed original, not that Nikki Blonsky display), there's something on the list for everyone.

I've found that a good old-fashioned movie night is one of the best and most practical ways to bond with my nieces and nephews. When we're all back home and the adults have gone to bed, we like to get into our pajamas, pop some popcorn, and cuddle up on the couch with a good flick. It's important to let them take turns choosing the movies as well, but when it's your turn, make it count.

## ☐ Go on a shopping spree

Fashion and style are some of the most important forms of self-expression. Whether they're leaning toward designer or vintage, mainstream or avant-garde, help them explore their aesthetic. But at the end of the day, make sure they know it's what's on the inside that defines them.

I had the chance to partake in some retail therapy with Cassie during her first trip to New York, when I played tour guide. She wanted to do Fifth Avenue, but I was more of a SoHo boy. So, we compromised and did both.

### ☐ Help them develop a skin care routine

Admittedly, this hasn't always been a priority for me—my sister Joan was actually the one who guilted me into starting my own routine. All you need are the basics (which is still about all my knowledge of skin care), including a cleanser, a toner, and a moisturizer. I also like to add an undereye cream before the moisturizer, because I have more bags than Louis Vuitton.

On that note, a mani/pedi or a facial is always a fun and fruitful outing for a day with the guncle. Treat them to a light spa day if you have the resources, or just buy some Korean facemasks from your local Ulta and pamper yourselves at home. All that matters are the 15 to 20 minutes of chill bonding time as your pores are being cleaned.

### ☐ Get them politically active

Make sure they're registered to vote, and even help them with the process if you have to. But more importantly, make sure they understand the importance of their voice. This shouldn't be much of a problem, as I find most Gen-Z kids have created their own forms of empowerment.

As important as it is to try to instill a sense of social and political responsibility, you can do so without campaigning for a particular candidate. Sure, there's one particular "politician" we can hopefully all agree doesn't deserve our support. But it's more important to help your nieces and nephews develop their own sense of judgment than to tell them who to vote for. You can present them with the facts and challenges faced by marginalized communities without telling them how they should think. If you do your job right, they'll hopefully make the right decisions on their own when the time comes.

## *Ages 21+*

### ☐ **Take them to a drag show**

Drag has been a powerful form of representation for generations, and in recent years, it's made its way into the mainstream. RuPaul Charles broke down barriers with the trailblazing competition reality series *RuPaul's Drag Race,* earning him several Emmy Awards. And since then, there's been an emergence of drag queen story hours across the country, as well as the first drag queen candidate for elected office with one of my favorite New York queens (and favorite human beings in general) Marti Gould Cummings.

Although I haven't had a chance to check this off my list yet, I have got my sister Joan hooked on *RuPaul's Drag Race,* which she's begun watching with her daughters almost as religiously as I do. And there's always an open invitation to take her and the girls to a drag show at the local gay bar when we're all back home in Jackson.

### ☐ **Take them to bottomless brunch**

If straight people have all-you-can-eat buffets, gays have laid claim to bottomless brunch. It's a favorite pastime for any millennial with the slightest bit of culture. Instead of church, we congregate over mimosas and Bellinis at Sunday brunch.

This is obviously an experience that should be reserved until everyone involved is of legal age. I had the pleasure of taking my oldest niece Cassie to bottomless brunch when she and her boyfriend visited me in New York City. It was a nice lowkey reunion in which we reconnected over some huevos rancheros and all the booze we wanted, taking family bonding to the next level.

## ☐ Take them to get tested

It's never a comfortable moment, especially to share with someone you're related to. But given that most straight parents might shirk this responsibility when the time comes, it lies on the guncle to teach them the importance. And it's crucial to do so from a place of education, not judgment.

Getting tested is important for everyone, not just LGBTQ people. And in most cities, there are usually resources for free testing, which often go vastly underutilized. It only takes a few minutes, and the sense of satisfaction from knowing your status outweighs the momentary cringe by far.

## ☐ Take them to Stonewall

This would require a trip to New York City and a 21st birthday, but it's definitely worth it when the opportunity arises. There's usually a good drag show going on upstairs, and there are more than enough fun queer spots down Christopher Street (including Julius, the city's oldest gay bar, which happens to serve one of the best burgers in New York) to include this place on a good barhop.

More than just a bar, Stonewall is still and will always be an important cornerstone for the LGBTQ community of New York City, if not the world. As a queer person, seeing the birthplace of the modern queer equality movement is probably the equivalent of Christians visiting Jerusalem. There's an overwhelming amount of history to be admired.

I made the very conscious choice to have my first (legal) drink at Stonewall when I turned 21 during my summer internship at *OUT Magazine*. Such a seminal moment deserved to take place in a location of historic significance.

## All Ages

☐ **Prioritize their mental health**

Growing up in my family, we never talked too much about our emotions. It's not that I was deprived of affection or anything, but we just didn't quite know how to express all our feelings in a healthy away. So, things like mental health were never much of a priority.

Try to establish yourself as a safe person for your nieces and nephews to come to with anything they're feeling, and make sure they don't feel judged. Or if you don't feel equipped to handle whatever they're going through, at least provide them with the resources to find someone who is. At the very least, offer yourself as an interpreter of sorts who can relay their struggles to their parents if that's what they want or need, but do so mindfully as not to break their trust.

☐ **Offer them a sex positive sounding board**

Lesbi-honest, the "birds and the bees" talk with parents will always be awkward. And as long as straight parents refer to it as the "birds and the bees" talk, they likely won't have the necessary resources to guide such a conversation. Goddess knows the public school systems in this country aren't much help either.

It's a sticky situation (no pun intended), and nobody wants to start that talk. But it's important to at least let them know that they have a nonjudgmental sounding board for any of their burning questions (still no pun intended). Once again, at least offer them the proper resources if the conversation is too uncomfortable for either party or if you feel you don't have all the answers.

#### ☐ Volunteer with them

While you can't help but want to spoil your nieces and nephews at every opportunity, it's also important to give them a sense of duty toward their fellow human. Volunteering is a chance to not only introduce them to some of the causes close to your heart, but also to help motivate them in their own philanthropic interests.

And it can still be a fun activity, as opposed to some dreaded moral obligation. Get creative with how you donate your time and what causes you donate to. One of the best times I've had giving back was making personalized Christmas stockings and filling them with thoughtful gifts for a group home that housed LGBTQ kids in the foster system.

#### ☐ Build their self-esteem

As queer people, we remember all too well the cruel sense of not feeling good enough that comes with growing up. Adolescence is hard enough without being confronted with unrealistic standards of beauty and strictly defined gender roles. Every child deserves to pave their own path of self-discovery with the carefree confidence that's so often stolen from us at an early age.

It's a guncle's job to break down those walls and teach his nieces and nephews that there's no right or wrong answer to the question of their identity. For every potential judgmental look or rude Instagram comment they might face, it's our responsibility to build them up.

### ☐ Be your true self

Building their self-esteem is so important, but the most effective way to show them that they can be confident in themselves is to be just as confident in yourself. At nearly thirty years old, I still know that's much easier said than done. Middle school bullies don't stay in middle school, but as you get older, you develop a thicker skin.

I admit that I try to avoid preachy moments with my own nieces and nephews, as our unique dynamic doesn't always call for it. But from everything they and their parents tell me, kids pick up on the little details, and they learn from them. I'm one of the few people in my family who deviated from the married-with-kids-after-high-school life plan, opting to chase my dreams and be my true self, and that's an impression that sticks.

# Chapter 4

# GUNCLE DON'T PREACH

Coming out wasn't an easy process for me. I don't think it ever is. I recognize that it was a much easier experience than most have faced—many LGBTQ people's families disown them entirely. But I was still coming out to a mostly conservative family in the south who'd been whispering microaggressions under their breaths about queer people my whole life. Although their thinking has progressed over the years, no cisgender heterosexual person can truly understand what a lonely experience it can be.

Like most in my situation, I'd always wished I had just one person in my family who knew what I was going through. The only gay family member I had was a second cousin who'd moved to Las Vegas before I was born to work as a drag queen, and although we never met, I'd at least admired him for getting out from the socially constricted confines of Jackson when he did. But every story I was told about him felt like a cautionary tale, as he was often equated to the disappointment of his convicted felon brother.

The closest person in my family who accepted me unconditionally was my older sister Joan. But being that she lived three states away, and I only saw her once a year at most, I'd already come out to the rest of my family and started to find my own form of self-acceptance by the time I was able to have a face-to-face conversation with her.

Having so many nieces and nephews, I'd only hoped that if one of them was going through what I did, I could be to them what I'd so desperately needed.

Blake P, an animator in Los Angeles, recently experienced this first-hand when his 12-year-old nephew came out to him as gay. Also from a conservative southern family, everyone he'd told just chalked it up to being a phase. That's why it was so important that he had a guncle like Blake who he could turn to, someone who'd already experienced the struggle of being queer in their family. He told me, "Him reaching out to me, me being that person for him felt incredible. I've had a very tumultuous relationship with my family—I was the only gay person. So, having him come out to me felt like I had a family again."

Don't mistake this sense of compassion with an attempt to recruit or convert anyone. If anything, it's an instinctive need to protect future generations, perhaps making the pain of coming out feel less in vain. Some scientists credit the kin selection hypothesis, which says that gay men are biologically hardwired to nurture and help raise the children of their siblings and other relatives, thereby helping perpetuate their own genes.

And although gaydar is a scientifically unproven method, it's not unheard of that a queer person might sense familiar traits in someone else, particularly someone in their own family. Nick Fager says, "More often than not, they are picking up on something very real in a family member. My belief is that a very small percentage of the population is completely straight and cisgender by traditional definitions, so it's almost a guarantee that someone in your family has experienced queer feelings."

During Key West Pride a few years ago, I had the pleasure of meeting Stuart Milk, the nephew of gay trailblazer Harvey Milk. It also happened to be the weekend of the Pulse nightclub shooting in 2016. It was a tragedy that shook our community to the core, and being three hours away during a massive queer celebration at the time it happened, the emotions were particularly raw.

As a gay man himself, Stuart had long been carrying on his uncle's legacy as co-founder of the Harvey Milk Foundation. Just hours after

*All young people, regardless of sexual orientation or identity, deserve a safe and supportive environment in which to achieve their full potential.*

—Harvey Milk
(activist, politician, guncle)

news of the shooting broke, he led a vigil as hundreds of LGBTQ people in town for Pride marched to the sea. He took his spot at the end of a dock, where he gave an empowering speech to a crowd of queer people and allies, packed shoulder to shoulder. In attempt to get a better spot, I walked through the water to watch from the side through people's legs, a moment I fondly recall when times feel particularly distressing for our community.

I'd always admired the legacy left by Harvey Milk. He clearly inspired many when they were at their lowest, and seeing someone he influenced on such a personal level gave me perspective not only on my role as a guncle, but also as an example for any young person.

## Guncle Wisdom

Being a role model doesn't mean standing on a soapbox and lecturing your nieces and nephews on right and wrong. How does that saying go? Oh yes, "You can lead a horse to water, but children aren't horses, so why are we comparing them?"

Kids are smarter than we often give them credit for, and they're quite observant of their environment. Instead of preaching to them, live your life by example, and they will surely notice. Trust me, I've learned this the hard way.

Ironically, the only one of my nieces and nephews I felt could benefit from the guidance I so instinctively wanted to offer was already fortunate enough to have a progressive mom of her own. Kayla wasn't officially a family member but a close family friend that I'd known since I was born and often considered another sister, subsequently seeing her children as nieces.

Her daughter Penny was always such an introvert. Getting more than a couple of words out of her was often like trying to have an exchange with a Twitter bot. It didn't help that when they visited, I was typically the only male presence in a house full of women who didn't quite know how to appreciate the perks of having a gay family member.

With my other nieces, it was usually easy to bond with them, if not ending up in a childish spat here and there. With Penny, I never quite knew where I stood. Frequently one to get lost in my own insecurities, I was often convinced she just didn't like me. But it was actually just how she acted with everyone, a fact her mother would tell you.

My aunt once casually compared Penny to "Elvira" (the Oak Ridge Boys song, not the mistress of the dark), which she thought had offended her. But that was just Penny's natural demeanor, something I could ultimately relate to, having been born with resting bitch face. If I wasn't actively excited about something, it was easy to confuse my contentment with disappointment, something that often prompted my mom to persistently drill me with one "what's wrong?" after another.

As I grew older, I began to resonate with Penny's self-prescribed isolation. Coming to terms with my sexuality made me feel like an outsider in my own family. Therefore, it made Penny feel more like a kindred spirit than ever, lost among the people who knew us best.

And perhaps it was wishful thinking, not necessarily that

she was queer, but the idea of knowing I wasn't the only one. Over the years, I couldn't help but wonder if she was going through the same struggles I once experienced. I'd never wish that on anyone, but if it was the case, I wanted to be someone she could turn to, which I never had.

It wasn't just her introverted behavior that gave me suspicions. People in the south would probably describe Penny as a tomboy. A more woke person might say she didn't conform to gender stereotypes.

Years of her basketball team portraits collaged our refrigerator door back home. It didn't help that she never had a boyfriend nor even seemed to show interest in boys growing up (granted, she never expressed an interest in girls, either). It didn't quite occur to me at the time, but these were the same stereotypes or "clues" people saddled me with as a child, which I'd always wished I could escape.

When I finally came out, several family members and friends made sure to let me know they would have suspected a particular cousin of mine was gay before me. Although perhaps that was a well-intentioned statement, it still made me feel as if being perceived as queer was something to be ashamed of. It was also unfair to my cousin to make assumptions about their identity behind their back, which gave me the biting insecurity that my own family could be so insensitive.

I ultimately came to realize that—like I didn't appreciate these particular family members doing—it wasn't my place to form suspicions about her identity. Having gone through that terrifying uncertainty and loneliness myself, I didn't want to project my insecurities about being queer in our family onto Penny—or anyone. Not only was the reasoning just rooted in outdated stereotypes, but her self-discovery was her own, not a tool to make me feel validated. All I could do was offer her support the best way I knew how.

Fager adds, "Of course, it isn't our job to out anyone except ourselves, so the best way to deal with this is simply to live authentically as yourself, and by doing this you give people around you permission to do the same. And if you notice that the more authentic you get, the more a certain family member distances, then that is a clear sign to start investing less energy in that person, even if that brings up a great deal of sadness."

While I couldn't help but be curious, I tried to make it a point not to steal any potential moment from her or make her feel pressured to choose an identity. I made what I hoped was a subtle effort to ensure she felt comfortable talking to me about those kinds of things. It was disguised as a casual chat I brought up once with her and one of her siblings during one of their visits when they rode along with me to Little Caesars to pick up pizza for the family.

Although I tried to bring it up in a natural way, it was probably about as graceful as a teen pregnancy announcement at a Pentecostal church gathering. But I had to throw it out there to give my inner closeted child a sense of peace, "You know if any of you ever had trouble coming to terms with your sexuality or anything like that, you could come to me, right?" It was casually met with the indifference of a handful of pre-teen voices mumbling "yeah" or "okay" without looking up from their phones.

Fager also recommends discussing the very real possibility of having a queer kid to their parents. He says, "I think it is helpful to simply pose the scenario to your siblings and their spouses. 'So, what if your kid turns out to be gay? Or trans? How will you handle that?'"

## Guncle Wisdom

Everyone goes through their own personal journeys of realizing their gender identity and sexuality, which cannot be forced or defined by others. When you out someone or even ask them if they're queer, they're forced to face a part of themselves that they've likely been made to feel shame over. That's not always easy for people who don't have a solid support system.

Instead of asking someone you love to define their identity, let them know that they have someone to help them discover who they are, and that you'll love them regardless of the outcome. Better yet, provide an example by living your own life honestly and openly, showing them that there's nothing to be ashamed of.

He adds, "This is not to put them on the spot, but rather to make them more conscious of the possibility. Many straight parents simply don't consciously think about the possibility, and therefore they let their unconscious bias affect their kids in ways they don't even realize."

But as Penny got older, I saw her come out of her shell and feel more comfortable in her own skin. I can even see it in the selfies she posts to Instagram, that there's real happiness behind her smile, not just the typical obligation to put on a happy face for the camera. That's something I'm not even sure I've managed to accomplish in my twenty-eight years.

Last time I saw her, I met her first boyfriend, someone who actually seems to have put her at ease. We had a chance to bond at her birthday party in Little Rock in a way that felt more natural than I'm used to with most of my family. It was almost like meeting her for the first time, now that we've both evolved to a sense of comfort in our own identities.

We eventually had a discussion about her journey with self-acceptance, which ultimately resulted in her rejecting societal ideals of gender norms and embracing her own version of womanhood. I'd never been prouder as a guncle, and I was touched that she felt comfortable opening up about that experience.

I'd like to say it was surprising to learn how self-aware Penny turned out to be, a quality I still often lack. But if I'm being honest, I've always seen a level of emotional maturity in her and all my nieces and nephews that I could never hold a light to.

## Takeaways

- Establish yourself as a safe space for nieces and nephews to discuss sexuality.
- Don't project your own past struggles onto them; let them make those discoveries themselves.
- Children are smart, so live your life by example and they'll pick up on that.
- Prepare your siblings for the possibility that their children might identify as LGBTQ.

# Chapter 5

# HIP TO BE GUNCLE

**B**eing a guncle usually comes with an unspoken cool factor. Perhaps it's the fact that we know every word of their favorite musical *Hairspray*, and the movie's cult classic roots in the 1988 John Waters-helmed original version. Maybe it's because we're experts at nailing the perfect birthday gift that came from our cultural understanding of their blossoming interest in Jimmy Choo over Forever 21. But more likely, it's the moments we share, those unique experiences that take the curiosity of someone that never felt appeased by the typical heteronormative routines.

RJ Kennedy, who moonlights as recording artist Ginger O'Nasty, found a bonding moment in a rare form. He recalled, "I do have a song out on iTunes called 'Hey Gurl' by Dorian Wyld featuring myself, and it's a flamboyant bop that my nephews all seem to love at a young age. My demographic was really supposed to be for club bangers, but for some reason kids love to 'yass kween' and 'hey gurl!'"

I've honestly never felt like the cool uncle, as my older siblings often seemed to win my nieces' and nephews' affection when we were all together. There were still those subtle moments of unique comradery, like when Cassie and her friends painted my toenails after I fell asleep on the couch (okay, maybe that's more hazing than comradery). But as I grew up and came into my own identity, I think my sense of confidence and self-love rubbed off on them to fortify a much deeper bond.

Even before I began to satisfy my appetite for queer culture, I often managed to meet my oldest nieces in their comfort zone (which turned out to be my comfort zone as well, even if I wasn't ready to admit it). When we would visit, I would try to convince them (unsuccessfully) it was their idea that we play with Barbies and watch Mary-Kate and Ashley movies.

Later when I started my first job at Malco Grandview Theater and got free movie tickets every week, I began the tradition of taking them to such classics as *Hannah Montana: The Movie* and *A Bad Moms Christmas*. Unfortunately, our trips didn't line up with some of the more obvious gay choices of the past couple of decades like *Love, Simon* or at least the gay favorites like *Burlesque*. Those came with midnight runs to the local Redbox or Netflix binges after the rest of the adults went to sleep. How else would I introduce my impressionable nephew Nico to such (not necessarily queer, but still seminal) classics like *Little Monsters* (the 1989 Fred Savage flick) or *Mighty Morphin Power Rangers: The Movie*?

When I visited them in South Carolina one year around Halloween, I played the cool uncle by driving Cassie, Dakota, and their friends to a haunted house and hayride about an hour away. As I was more an enthusiast of real scares over church members in Walmart-bought masks, I opted to take a detour on the way back to a haunted cemetery I found online. It was the middle of the night when we arrived at the creepy, nondescript spot in the woods, where all we saw was another parked car before freaking out and immediately leaving.

## Guncle Wisdom

Spoiling your nieces and nephews doesn't have to mean dropping wads of cash on Broadway shows or the hot new toy, which they'll likely get bored with in a week. It's the little bonding moments that they'll take with them, regardless of the price tag.

If you want to connect with them, share the things you love in life. The most precious gift you can give them is the time spent together. They'll treasure those moments for years to come.

By the time Cassie graduated high school, I decided to up the ante for some classic guncle/niece bonding. By that time, I was out of the closet and preparing to travel back to New York for an internship at *Teen Vogue*. It would be the summer that birthed the rise of the influencer and with it, my misguided attempt to establish myself as a fashion blogger, influenced partially by the rich kids who secured their coveted spots through nepotism.

Although it was really a gift from Joan, since she funded it, I offered to bring Cassie along for the first week, after my mom, Devyn, and I drove into town to see her graduate.

When we arrived in South Carolina, Cassie brought me up to her room to show me something. She pulled a box out of her closet, filled with her collection of *Teen Vogue* back issues. It was often difficult to gauge if my parents were proud of me when I was truly excited about achievements like these, but that moment was the first time I felt like someone else was just as excited as I was.

My internship wasn't set to start until after Cassie returned home, which meant I could devote a full week to showing her my favorite city. We shared a futon (sleeping foot to face) in Brooklyn at the Bed-Stuy apartment of my friend Anthony, which was crawling with a litter of kittens

their cat had recently birthed. Anthony, a go-go dancer and former professional ballerina I met the previous summer who quickly became my best friend, lived in the fourth-floor walkup with his scientist fiancé Seth.

It was past midnight when we arrived in Brooklyn, but Cassie and I were still awake. So, I decided to introduce her to the F train for a 2:00 a.m. excursion to Times Square, the only time when you can enjoy the lights without squeezing through a sea of tourists. We stopped by the then-Condé Nast building as a run-through for my soon-to-be daily commute, before splitting some chicken nuggets at the nearby 24-hour McDonalds.

During her stay, I gave her the classic New York experience with a trip to the top of the Empire State Building and an introduction to the bodega cats of the city. She almost experienced the New York rite of passage that is getting off the train at the wrong stop, before she turned around to see I was still seated. The only thing we didn't manage to do was take in a Broadway show.

Musical theater is actually one of the regular bonding moments for my friend Daniel Franzese, star of *Mean Girls* and *Looking*, and his nieces. He fondly told me, "I knew one of my major jobs as a guncle was to make sure she knew Broadway musicals. When my niece Italina was five years old, I took her to see *Gypsy*, and she just danced and enjoyed the show, but doesn't remember it at all because she was too young. Now, she is the perfect age!"

He added, "This is where my role as guncle really comes in. I want to spoil my niece, this is true. Even more than that, I want her to have all the cultural benefits and child-like humor that we as queer people possess."

Although Broadway wasn't on the list, I did manage to introduce Cassie to a little bit of the city's vast gay culture. We took a stroll through the West Village, where I showed her the historic Stonewall Inn, though she couldn't yet get in. Anthony and I later took her to the now-shuttered 18-and-older Splash Bar, which was also my first New York gay bar experience, as well as where Anthony used to strut half naked on the bar for tips. It turned out to be a dead night, in which the shirtless bartender tried to charge me four bucks for a bottle of water, but we had the time of our lives.

It also turned out to be a moment of cultural enlightenment that Cassie craved, which her par-

*Try and understand what part you have to play in the world in which you live. There's more to life than you know, and it's all happening out there. Discover what part you can play, and then go for it.*

—Ian McKellen
(actor, guncle)

ents also encouraged. There are gay bars in just about every metropolitan area across the 50 free states, but the farther south you go, the more hidden away they are (with the exceptions of tourist meccas like Miami and New Orleans). Being in a place like New York, where there are entire neighborhoods devoted to and embracing queer community, sheds a beautiful light on that kind of love and acceptance that's nearly blinding for someone growing up in South Carolina or Mississippi.

Johnny Sibilly has a similar experience in his bond with his own niece. "As a gay uncle, for some reason I've always felt a special bond with my niece, because I've known her before the world could force any opinions of who I was on her. That is special. It's always felt like a breath of fresh air to think, *Here's an opportunity for a little human to get to know me exactly as I am.*"

## Guncle Wisdom

Meet them in their comfort zone. It's tempting to want to curate the perfect bonding moments as a proud guncle. But it's also important to validate their interests, no matter what age range they're for.

Just as you would enthusiastically answer a toy phone a toddler hands you, you should show that enthusiasm in their interests, no matter what age. That includes when your preteen nephew wants to watch WWE. Consider it an honor that they want to include you in their world.

Cassie graced me with another visit a few years later when I was settled into my life as a full-time New York resident (way up in Washington Heights) and as an assistant editor at *OUT Magazine*. She was visiting her boyfriend (who later became her husband) Carter while he was attending SUNY Maritime. It was my first time meeting her boyfriend, who'd already won over the rest of the family when they went back to visit my mom on an occasion when I couldn't make it home.

As we were finally all of drinking age, I jumped at the opportunity to introduce them to one of my favorite New York pastimes, bottomless brunch. Several Bellinis in, I could see what she saw in her high school sweetheart, her perfect match.

After a boozy brunch, we shuffled from the East Village on up to Chelsea for more booze. I introduced them to one of my favorite local gay staples, Gym Bar. Although it was a gay bar, it was also a sports bar with plenty of exposed natural light, which seemed a safe compromise for a straight boy from South Carolina. Not that it was my intention to test his reaction to such a spot, but I was pleasantly surprised at his nonchalance toward a community at which many of his peers might scoff.

As my nieces and nephews get older, the personal moments come more easily. I've started a group text with a few of them, trying to keep up with their lives. I even share a drink with the ones who are of age, when we get the chance, a bonding experience I wish I could have with everyone I love.

Not to get too religious on you, but if God does exist, she created the guncle to fill a role that many can't in children's lives. While to some, we may just seem like the cool family member, there's a bond that goes much deeper than most with our heterosexual counterparts.

Franco De Marco echoed that sentiment, "I think that they get a lot of my extra attention. They bring a legit joy and happiness to my face."

He added, "As a trans man, I never thought I would live to the age I am now: breaths from 30, thriving, and close with my immediate family. My bond with my sister has gotten me through some of my roughest years. And in some of my darkest days, I think of those two little precious ones, and everything just lights back up."

## *Takeaways*

- Being the cool guncle doesn't have to mean dropping a bunch of cash on spoiling them.
- The most memorable moments don't come with a price tag, but a fond shared experience.
- As a guncle, you have a unique opportunity to be a role model in their lives.

# Chapter 6

# THE WISDOM OF GUNCLE

Although guncle-hood is filled with endless bonding moments, it comes with the responsibility to educate a new generation. Straight parents often simply don't have the tools to provide their children with realistic expectations of what the world is like for people who don't benefit from cisgender heterosexual white male privilege. It's just not something they have to think about, and therefore don't prepare for it.

Johnny Sibilly managed to educate his niece in epic fashion. He said, "I do remember us going to get manis and pedis and her saying at age four, 'Boys don't get their nails done!' And I responded, 'Taking care of your hands and feet is for both boys and girls. It doesn't belong to one gender!' She looked confused but she also never questioned our mani/pedi moments again."

I had a similar moment with my nephew Nico a few years ago. We were all playing the board game Life, and I opted for two blue pegs in my car, something I was proud to be able to do at the family dinner table. Nico exclaimed, "You can't have two boys get married!" As I was under the impression his parents already told him, I tried to explain that I was gay, and that's how I would live my life. But being much younger and possibly more introverted than I, he didn't seem open to that chat.

It's not always easy to lead a horse to water. But kids today often make an effort to educate themselves and others, leading the way in social progress (with the help of major strides made by past generations).

Not long ago, I met my niece Beck's boyfriend. Admittedly, I might have formed some premature judgments of him when she told me he belonged to their high school's conservative club. I tried not to hold it against him, as I considered myself a conservative at that age as well (a product of my environment).

When I asked Beck if she was a conservative too, she said she didn't know what she was. "I'm not old enough to vote yet, so it doesn't matter," she told me. It was hard not to feel a little disheartened at that justification. And although the thought of her aligning herself with the conservatives of this country was heartbreaking, I was more concerned that she didn't seem to have an opinion at all.

I wanted to tell her that her opinion was just as important as anyone else's, regardless of whether or not she could vote. But I could tell she seemed uncomfortable with the conversation, and I didn't want to violate the cardinal rule of my family and most families of mixed political affiliations: "Don't discuss politics." I might have been one of the few to actually observe that rule in my family, but being outnumbered as one of the few liberals, it was often easier to just grin and bear it.

Beck was one of the lucky ones, though. My sister Joan parented her with a more infor-

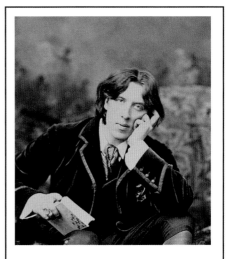

*Education is an admirable thing. But it is well to remember from time to time that nothing that is worth knowing can be taught.*

—Oscar Wilde
(writer, guncle)

mative view of the world than I felt our parents provided us. She might not identify herself an outright liberal, but she at least had a strong enough moral compass to gauge the good from the bad in this world.

Against my better judgment, I recently brought up the subject again. It was Beck's eighteenth birthday, and I sent her the obligatory "happy birthday" text message (one of the few times I remembered anyone's birthday). But I also took the opportunity to remind her that she was now old enough to vote. "I know! It's kind of scary and exciting," she texted back.

She definitely hit the nail on the head. I think I can recall feeling that same sinking feeling of sudden duty that came with my newfound adulthood. But in my situation, I shrugged the responsibility of declaring a political stance until it all just became crystal clear (and since I turned eighteen shortly after the 2008 election, I had plenty of time to get there).

Going to high school in Mississippi, my view was clouded by the ignorance and bigotry that surrounded me, perpetuated by generations before. When it came to issues like same-sex marriage, I took the opposing view as default, in fear that my support would give away my identity that I hadn't even fully discovered yet. In most cases, it was just easier to take an impartial stance.

> ## Guncle Wisdom
>
> Remain cognizant of opportunities to educate your nieces and nephews, but don't force it. They'll have plenty of questions for you, but it's best to let them ask before you answer.
>
> It's better to be available for them when they need you than to impose your knowledge where you see fit. It may be necessary at times but tread lightly. You gain their trust by being the sounding board they know they can turn to.

It wasn't until going off to college in Flagstaff, Arizona, that everything just clicked. That little mountain town was a liberal exception to the rest of the red state. I was quickly elected to the school's gay-straight alliance (GSA), and I surrounded myself with queer people, liberal people, and people who I could see eye-to-eye with.

It never quite dawned on me that Beck was just going through the same thing. She told me she hadn't aligned herself with a particular political stance, because she felt too manipulated by her environment. She didn't want her opinion to be influenced by the opinions of others, which was why she didn't discuss politics with her boyfriend.

Ultimately, she still found politics confusing (something I could still resonate with in my late twenties). During a time when teens and young people feel so empowered to stand strong in their beliefs, she was unsure of which politicians could actually be trusted, especially living in the south, where most people are set in their views (no matter how ignorant). It's hard not to respect that kind of reservation when many feel inclined to declare their beliefs at every available outlet.

RJ Kennedy also considers the growing social responsibility of young people to be a product of their generation, which is hard to deny. He says: "I also think it's a sign of the times that kids are growing up in a different social atmosphere than we did when we were younger. I wasn't exposed to an LGBT person at a young age, and it wasn't normal for me to see two guys walking down the street holding hands."

He added: "Nowadays, the tables have turned, and kids just don't question what's deemed normal or not normal. They just want to know when they are getting their electronics back. I feel like if a parent doesn't make a big deal about something in front of a child, the child doesn't pick up on it."

As I said, the small minds of my hometown were one of the driving reasons for me to get out as soon as I could. It was honestly the only way I thought I could live a happy and full life. And that tenacity for finding a place to belong apparently rubbed off on my niece Dakota.

She noticed my strong will to leave home for greener

pastures, which showed her she doesn't have to stick around the place she grew up if it's not the place she wants to end up. Ultimately, she wants to live either on the beach in South Carolina or in the mountains of North Carolina to stay close to her parents, an instinct I understand, as I'm often overcome with a feeling of homesickness, regardless of my hometown's flaws.

And although she's a southern girl at heart, she's developed an undeniable appetite for travel. She's actually been on several trips that made me more than a little jealous. In high school she took a class trip to Greece, a destination she hopes to return to in the future. And most recently, she stayed in the rainforests of Ecuador for her environmental science major.

Travel and politics weren't the only area in which I influenced them, as my coming out helped Dakota view those different from her without judgment or prejudice. It sounds like a basic enough level of compassion but growing up in the south often instills a sense of misguided intolerance. Although she and Beck both credited me with that piece of enlightenment, their parents have always led them with a solid moral compass.

Simon Dunn is still helping build that moral compass in his nephews. He said, "The youngest are two twin boys, and one likes to wear dresses occasionally. My experiences in life gave me the opportunity to educate his siblings to be more accepting. Obviously, being boys, they tease him, which is something their mother (my sister) reports back to me so I can speak with them about it."

## Guncle Wisdom

Imparting your worldly wisdom on the next generation is an important responsibility as a guncle. But make sure you know where their parents stand on the issues, and respect if they don't want you discussing certain things with their kids, regardless of how crucial it is.

On that note, don't turn your nieces and nephews against their parents. If they're coming to you because their mom and dad don't understand, they only need you to assure them that you do understand. It would only cause more problems than necessary to actively take sides against your siblings when it comes to their kids.

## Takeaways

- Remain cognizant of opportunities to educate your nieces and nephews.
- Try not to push them out of their comfort zone when it comes to discussing important topics.
- If you're unsure, defer to their parents about what conversations they're okay with their children having.

# THE ESSENTIAL GUNCLE VIEWING LIST

I've always had a profound love for movies, which presented infinite possibilities in life for a gay boy from Mississippi, whether running away to a big city or living his truth in his own identity.

My first job was at a movie theater, where I took advantage of every comped ticket. And I've since gone on to write about movies, interviewing the likes of Jane Fonda, Jennifer Lopez, and RuPaul Charles. I even came within two feet of Meryl Streep once at a press conference.

I still find my generation and Gen-Z's dependence on screens unfortunate. But my fondest memories with my nieces and nephews have been just cuddling up around the TV to watch some influential titles. I've often felt somewhat challenged as a potentially formative figure in their lives, but if there's one piece of quality wisdom I can pass on to them, it's through my devout love for movies.

I had a particularly lax childhood when it came to MPAA ratings, so what was age-appropriate for me might not be for others. I recommend using best judgment and always checking with their parents first if you're unsure. God knows my sister Joan was less than pleased when I tried to show my nieces *A Nightmare on Elm Street* before any of them had hit puberty.

Some of these are pieces of cinema that can teach them the histories and culture of those different from them, hopefully imparting a sense of inclusion. Others are just campy classics that helped me and many others come into our own identities.

☐ *The Rocky Horror Picture Show* (1975)
**R, dir. Jim Sharman**
**Plot:** When the newly engaged Brad and Janet break down in the middle of a stormy night, they happen upon Dr. Frank-N-Furter's castle. During their visit, they witness a mad scientist's creation and the peculiar company he keeps.
**Why kids should see it:** This is another Halloween classic, and it's a musical, which means it's a fun time for everyone. And Tim Curry's sweet transvestite from Transsexual, Transylvania, is an iconic character that everyone should be well acquainted with.
**Best one-liner:** "I see you shiver with antici... pation." —Tim Curry as Dr. Frank-N-Furter

☐ *Pee-wee's Big Adventure* (1985)
**PG, dir. Tim Burton**
**Plot:** When Paul Reubens' iconic titular character has his bike stolen, he sets off on a cross-country adventure to get it back, where he encounters a series of unforgettable characters.
**Why kids should see it:** Pee-wee Herman has long been an icon among the queer community, presenting an innocent sense of ambiguity to kids learning to be themselves.
**Best one-liner:** "I know you are, but what am I?" —Paul Reubens as Pee-wee Herman

☐ *Labyrinth* (1986)
**PG, dir. Jim Henson**
**Plot:** Jennifer Connelly plays Sarah, a typical angsty teenager whose disdain for her baby brother leads her on a quest to rescue the infant from the Goblin King Jareth (expertly portrayed by music icon David Bowie). She treks through a dangerous maze of nefarious obstacles and interesting creatures along her way.

**Why kids should see it:** You're never too young to be introduced to the seminal works of Bowie, whose androgynous sense of style made the Goblin King one of the most iconic characters in history.

**Best one-liner:** "You remind me of the babe." —David Bowie as Goblin King Jareth

☐ *Elvira: Mistress of the Dark* (1988)

**PG-13, dir. James Signorelli**

**Plot:** This is one of those perfect Halloween movies for those who aren't in for a scare. After the iconic cult-movie TV hostess Elvira finds out the great aunt she never knew she had has died, she heads off to New England, where evil forces stand between her and her inheritance.

**Why kids should see it:** In an era driven by so-called influencers, it's important to educate children on the cultural icons that paved the way, and Elvira's vampy valley girl is just that.

**Best one-liner:** "I've seen *The People's Court*. I'm entitled to one phone call and a strip search."—Cassandra Peterson as Elvira

☐ *Hairspray* (1988)

**PG, dir. John Waters**

**Plot:** Long before Nikki Blonsky and Zac Efron took on a much more Hollywood adaptation of the Broadway musical, John Waters released the cult classic source material. This mildly raunchy flick centers on a confident plus-sized teen in 1960s Baltimore who uses her platform on a local dance TV show to fight for racial equality.

**Why kids should see it:** In addition to the greatness that is John Waters' late drag queen muse Divine as Edna Turnblad, this movie also teaches an indispensable message of social responsibility.

**Best one-liner:** "Tracy, I have told you about that hair. All ratted up like a teenage Jezebel!" —Divine as Edna Turnblad

☐ *The Witches* (1990)
**PG, dir. Nicolas Roeg**
**Plot:** When he stumbles upon a conference of witches while on vacation with his grandmother, Luke overhears their plan to turn all the children into mice, shortly before they make him one of their victims. Now in rodent form, he must find a way to foil their nefarious plan.
**Why kids should see it:** Although Anjelica Huston wasn't taken seriously as an actress at the beginning of her career, this role proved her talent, and the children must be educated. It's also one of the few Halloween season classics that any age can enjoy, even if it's a little scary.
**Best one-liner:** "Everywhere I look, I see the repulsive sight of hundreds, thousands of revolting little children!" —Anjelica Huston as Grand High Witch

☐ *Don't Tell Mom the Babysitter's Dead* (1991)
**PG-13, dir. Stephen Herek**
**Plot:** When their mom takes off for an extended business trip, teenage Swell (played by Christina Applegate) tries to convince her mom she can take care of her four siblings for the summer. But when their strict babysitter unexpectedly croaks, she has to find a way to grow up quick and support her family.
**Why kids should see it:** This movie is filled with some important campy quotes and moments, thanks to a young Christina Applegate. And it also teaches the importance of discovering yourself without the help of your parents.
**Best one-liner:** "I'm right on top of that, Rose." —Christina Applegate as Swell

☐ *Death Becomes Her* (1992)
**PG-13, dir. Robert Zemeckis**
**Plot:** Meryl Streep and Goldie Hawn star as two old friends who go to extreme measures for eternal youth and beauty in their fight over the man of their dreams. But when they fail to read the fine print, they soon find out that the side effects outweigh the benefits.
**Why kids should see it:** This is aimed a bit more toward the older crowd, but it's a fun campy time that teaches an age-old message: "Beauty is skin deep."
**Best one-liner:** "*Now*, a warning?" —Meryl Streep as Madeline Ashton Menville

☐ *Sister Act 2: Back in the Habit* (1993)
**PG, dir. Bill Duke**
**Plot:** This is one of the few examples of a sequel that outshined the original, as Whoopi Goldberg's Deloris returns as Sister Mary Clarence to offer her guidance to a music class full of outcast Catholic students. With a prize performance from Lauryn Hill and a cameo from baby Jennifer Love Hewitt, this film is an instant classic.
**Why kids should see it:** Whoopi Goldberg is an icon for all ages, and her musical moments in this film are rivaled by few. It also preaches the idea of acceptance in a setting like the Catholic church, which often does not live up to that message.
**Best one-liner:** "If you want to be somebody, if you want to go somewhere, you better wake up and pay attention." —Whoopi Goldberg as Sister Mary Clarence

☐ *Hocus Pocus* (1993)
**PG, dir. Kenny Ortega**

**Plot:** Another Halloween classic, this one features an iconic cast of Bette Midler, Kathy Najimy, and Sarah Jessica Parker as the Sanderson sisters, three witch sisters who seek vengeance after a virgin unwittingly brings them back to life 300 years after they were hanged for sacrificing young children.

**Why kids should see it:** This has long been established as a seminal Halloween film, and it's obvious why, with its iconic cast and spooky/campy moments.

**Iconic queer moment:** Although not particularly queer, Sarah Jessica Parker singing her seductive hypnotic melody while hovering on a broomstick is engrained in the mind of every gay millennial.

☐ *Mixed Nuts* (1994)
**PG-13, dir. Nora Ephron**

**Plot:** A group of very different people (played by Steve Martin, Adam Sandler, Juliette Lewis, Rita Wilson, and more) in Venice Beach come into each other's lives on Christmas Eve, amid a series of disastrous moments. Don't worry, miracles do happen.

**Why kids should see it:** Although we've come to a point when there's no excuse not to cast trans people in trans roles, it was particularly progressive to have Liev Schreiber play a trans woman at the time. The movie was also one of my first examples of chosen family, and watching it has been a favorite Christmas tradition since I was a kid.

**Iconic queer moment:** Sandler's character Louie serenades Schreiber's Chris with a ukulele and a perfectly Sandler-esque song.

☐ *Gold Diggers: The Secret of Bear Mountain* (1995)
**PG, dir. Kevin James Dobson**
**Plot:** Christina Ricci plays Beth, a city girl who's reluctantly relocated to the mountains of Washington State with her mom, where she makes quick friends with outsider Jody (played by *My Girl* star Anna Chlumsky). The young women set off on an adventure into the taverns of Bear Mountain to find the gold hidden by local legend and pioneer Molly Morgan.
**Why kids should see it:** It's a pure movie about the friendship between two very different young women. But even I could pick up on the lesbian undertones from an early age, and it's the kind of movie that ushered many LGBTQ friends into their own paths of self-discovery.

☐ *To Wong Foo, Thanks for Everything! Julie Newmar* (1995)
**PG-13, dir. Beeban Kidron**
**Plot:** In an unlikely career move for the time, Patrick Swayze, Wesley Snipes, and John Leguizamo starred as three drag queens who go on a cross-country road trip to a drag pageant in Los Angeles. Along the way, they break down somewhere in the heartland, where they make some unexpected friendships.
**Why kids should see it:** My dad showed me this movie when I was four or five, and it stuck with me as one of my favorites over the years. Seeing this kind of mainstream queer representation, along with A-list actors, made it feel like being gay was something to be proud of.
**Best one-liner:** "Little Latin boy in drag, why are you crying? Maybe she just found out Menudo broke up." —Wesley Snipes as Noxeema Jackson

☐ *The First Wives Club* (1996)
**PG, dir. Hugh Wilson**

**Plot:** After their friend from college (Stockard Channing) succumbs to her depression, three divorced women (played by the iconic trio Diane Keaton, Goldie Hawn, and Bette Midler) vow to never let it happen to another woman. To make their vision happen, they must first seek out revenge on their ex-husbands.

**Why kids should see it:** It's the ultimate movie of female empowerment, filled with plenty of heartwarming moments that culminate in a win for the mothers, wives, and women we love.

**Iconic queer moment:** Diane Keaton, Goldie Hawn, and Bette Midler breaking out into song over Lesley Gore's "You Don't Own Me," dancing in the middle of the night through the streets of New York City, is one of the best movie endings of all time, and it offers an empowering battle cry for any marginalized group.

☐ *The Birdcage* (1996)
**R, dir. Mike Nichols**

**Plot:** The late Robin Williams and Nathan Lane star as a proud gay couple in Miami who must put on a hetero front to impress the uptight conservative family of their son's new fiancée. But with more than a few hiccups in their plan, some fabulous chaos ensues by the end of dinner.

**Why kids should see it:** LGBTQ representation was pretty scarce in films and television of the '90s. This movie offered a fun and rare look at the new normal of same-sex parents.

**Iconic queer moment:** Seeing past their differences, Williams and Lane manage to sneak Gene Hackman's Republican senator character out of the gay bar below their apartment by putting him in pure fish drag.

☐ *But I'm a Cheerleader* (1999)
**R, dir. Jamie Babbit**
**Plot:** One of Natasha Lyonne's breakout roles comes as Megan, a straitlaced young cheerleader whose parents send her to a conversion therapy camp after she starts showing signs of same-sex tendencies. (But this pray-the-gay-away retreat is a more stylized and colorful destination than you'd expect, with a fun cameo from RuPaul.) Instead of finding her way back to the straight and narrow, she finds comfort in the arms of Clea DuVall's Graham.
**Why kids should see it:** This should definitely be reserved for the older teen years, as it includes some mature themes. Having said that, it's a fun, campy time that offers a queer love story in an unexpected place.
**Iconic queer moment:** The ongoing flirtation between Lyonne and DuVall gets more and more passionate before culminating in their heartwarming ride off into the sunset.

☐ *Mean Girls* (2004)
**PG-13, dir. Mark Waters**
**Plot:** This movie stands the test of time as Lindsay Lohan's most iconic role and a fun time from start to finish. She starred as Cady Heron, a teenage girl acclimating to the cruel world of high school after being homeschooled in Africa for her whole life. With the help of two outsiders, she joins the Plastics, a clique of cool mean girls, with plans on taking them down from the inside.
**Why kids should see it:** The dark comedy has rarely been executed with such perfection, especially on such a relevant topic as high school hierarchy. No film gives a better education on how to treat your peers, especially the too-gay-to-function best friend.
**Best one-liner:** "She doesn't even go here!" —Daniel Franzese as Damian

☐ *Rent* (2005)

**PG-13, dir. Chris Columbus**

**Plot:** This Broadway musical classic centers on a group of struggling creatives in New York City for a year during the '80s. The diverse group of characters experiences life, love, and the tragedies that come with it, and it's all set to a soundtrack of showtunes every guncle should know by heart.

**Why kids should see it:** When queer history and the AIDS crisis are so often watered down in schools, this movie offers an emotionally raw look at life for LGBTQ people in the '80s, which every kid should learn about.

**Iconic queer moment:** Although there's romance and heartbreak aplenty for the queer characters in this movie, it's the song "Will I?" set in an AIDS support group that shines a necessary light on the tragedy that struck a generation.

☐ *The Family Stone* (2005)

**PG-13, dir. Thomas Bezucha**

**Plot:** When Everett Stone (Dermot Mulroney) brings his uptight girlfriend Meredith (Sarah Jessica Parker) home to meet his free-spirited family, she's subject to the scrutiny of his oddball brother (Luke Wilson), judgmental sister (Rachel McAdams), and skeptical mother (Diane Keaton).

**Why kids should see it:** One of my favorite family-friendly Christmas movies, it offers a glimpse at a modern family, in which the gay son is accepted with open arms, as well as his partner and their child.

**Iconic queer moment:** Diane Keaton goes into mama bear mode sticking up for her gay son when SJP's Meredith makes a problematic statement, a scene that still brings me to tears.

**Best one-liner:** "I love the gays!" —Sarah Jessica Parker as Meredith Morton

☐ *Burlesque* (2010)

**PG-13, dir. Steve Antin**

**Plot:** It's a classic story of a small-town girl with big dreams, starring Christina Aguilera as Ali, who runs off to Los Angeles to be a dancer. She finds herself at the famous Burlesque Lounge (super creative name, right?) where she attempts to prove herself to the boss, a tough-as-nails performer named Tess (expertly portrayed by Cher). As the establishment faces foreclosure, Ali saves the day with her insanely skilled vocal chops.

**Why kids should see it:** Amid the joyous amounts of shameless camp, this is ultimately a movie about chasing your dreams down and finding your chosen family. There's also plenty of epic musical numbers and Cher-isms that anyone can appreciate.

**Iconic queer moment:** Although not a card-carrying gay in real life, Stanley Tucci has earned an honorary spot in our community after playing not only Meryl Streep's GBF (gay best friend) in *The Devil Wears Prada*, but also starring as Cher's trusted gay Sean. Their beautiful friendship reminds us why the dynamic between girls and gay guys is so treasured.

**Best one-liner:** "Wagon wheel watusi!" —Cher as Tess

☐ *Philomena* (2013)
**PG-13, dir. Stephen Frears**
**Plot:** This tearjerker of a true story stars Dame Judi Dench as a woman who enlists the help of an investigative journalist in search of the son she was forced to give up 50 years before at a convent. During her search, she finds out her son is a proud gay man, but it's not a very happy ending.
**Why kids should see it:** Although Philomena never had the chance to meet her son, she accepted him fully for who he turned out to be. That's an important message for any kid.
**Iconic queer moment:** When discovering her long lost son was gay, Philomena's response was a nonchalant "I always knew that."

☐ *GBF* (2013)
**R, dir. Darren Stein**
**Plot:** The gay best friend has swept the nation as the hottest new accessory, but when the queen bees of North Gateway High School find their school seriously lacking the gay population, closeted teen Tanner is forced out of the closet. Although he enjoys the positive attention from his peers, he soon begins to feel like an object.
**Why kids should see it:** This is another rare example of a good queer teen film (regardless of its unfair R rating). It takes a step beyond the typical high school hierarchy and sheds a light on the struggles of trying to discover yourself when other people seem to have their minds made up about you.
**Iconic queer moment:** *Will & Grace* star Megan Mullally plays a mom who desperately wants to connect with her gay teen son, a bonding moment that ultimately comes in the form of an awkward *Brokeback Mountain* movie night.

☐ *Love, Simon* (2018)

**PG-13, dir. Greg Berlanti**

**Plot:** Simon is an average teenager who struggles with the decision to come out as gay when he falls for an anonymous pen pal. It becomes a romantic mystery as he tries to find out who his virtual Prince Charming is while attempting to keep his own secret.

**Why kids should see it:** This groundbreaking teen film offered a rare and needed sense of representation for a whole generation of LGBTQ kids, and it did so in a pure way that showed a real example of the gay adolescent experience with a happy ending.

**Iconic queer moment:** The kiss that takes place between Simon and his mystery beau at the end gave me more chills than the one in *Never Been Kissed*, particularly because of its trailblazing impact.

# Chapter 7

# A BROTHER
# AND A GUNCLE

While being a guncle often means providing what sage wisdom you can to your nieces and nephews, it also means imparting that wisdom on your brothers and sisters as they raise their children, and doing so in a way that doesn't overstep boundaries. It's every mom and dad's goal to be better parents than their own, even if they had the best childhood. And as the guncle is often the most socially progressive member of their family, it ends up being our job to bridge the gap between our own generation and the next.

I'd like to tell you this is a simple enough task, but the older a person gets, the more set in their ways they become. You can spout truths all day from your soapbox, but if they're not willing to learn, you might as well be yelling into a void.

R. Kurt Osenlund, an editor I had the pleasure of working with during my days at *OUT Magazine*, knows just as well as I do that you have to pick your battles. He says, "There are some issues that we

*If we desire a society in which men are brothers, then we must act towards one another with brotherhood. If we can build such a society, then we would have achieved the ultimate goal of human freedom.*

—Bayard Rustin
(activist, guncle)

discuss, of course, and we hear each other out. Sometimes we agree, sometimes we don't. Such is life. And my life experience is going to bring new things to their attention, just as their life experience will bring new things to mine."

I've been pretty fortunate to have a family that's been relatively susceptible to change. Although most of them had a somewhat predictable reaction to my coming out, they've managed to evolve to a place of understanding . . . or at least an attempt to be. But it didn't happen overnight.

Although with Joan, it actually happened pretty quickly, as she somehow managed to come out unscathed by the ignorance we were both subject to, growing up in the Bible Belt of Mississippi. She never ceases to amaze me with her unwavering compassion when it feels like the rest of the world has turned their backs on me. More importantly, she's never shy when it comes to being educated on things she doesn't understand, a quality most parents could stand to acquire.

When she suspected one of my nieces' soccer coaches might be a lesbian, she asked me how to find out. First, I told her the obvious,

"There's no trick to finding out if someone's gay, other than asking them." (But I also clarified that's not a recommended move because boundaries.) I followed it up by asking her if it really mattered. It wasn't a defensive response, just simple logic that doesn't often occur to those in heteronormative society, something she actually took into consideration as a teachable moment.

More recently, she called me after a trip to her local Ulta Beauty, where one of her favorite stylists was someone who didn't present as cisgender. This time, her question was regarding what gender pronouns to use. Once again, my answer was to ask, but only if it came up naturally. The question alone was something I'd never expect to hear from most of my family members.

## Guncle Wisdom

If your siblings are coming to you with questions, it means they're making an actual effort to educate themselves. There are no wrong questions, no matter how problematic, only wrong answers.

Don't respond to offensive questions with judgment, no matter how tempting it may be. They asked you because they trust you and value your opinion. Do your best to explain the underlying issues with whatever topic they've come to you with. Remember, they're your loved ones, not Twitter trolls attempting to get a rise out of you.

Although we weren't always as close as Joan and I were, Ollie made a noticeable effort to progress over the years. He still can't resist hitting me with a dose of life lessons during his sporadic long-distance lectures. But I have to admit that he's been open to my preaching as well, during the rare occasion I get the opportunity to educate him on queer culture. It's safe to assume that it's in large part thanks to his wife Chloe, who helped guide him through my coming out.

During one of my visits to see them, their twin boys Gavin and Gabe were playing dress-up, a pastime I fondly remember from my days of strutting around my preschool at Woodville Heights Baptist Church in the pink plastic heels from the Little Tikes princess set. I was pleasantly surprised to see Gavin go for the Batman costume, while Gabe opted for Wonder Woman. I was even more satisfied with Chloe's justification of letting her kids explore who they are, as opposed to the justification that came with my early years of gender expression. The twenty-something-year-old women who watched after us at daycare would laugh in amusement and chalk it up to, "He'll grow out of it."

With Devyn, it wasn't always as easy to appeal to her Christian senses, as she's always been a much more devout churchgoer than myself, even since childhood. When I first came out, I was satisfied enough with her response, "I don't agree with it, but I love you no matter what." It's more tolerance than most queer kids receive when revealing their truths.

It didn't immediately click that it was a common passive response from those who would vote against gay marriage but wouldn't tell a gay person to their face (unless separated by a picket line), "You're going to hell!" It did click a year or two later when I saw that she'd followed a Chick-fil-A support group on Facebook, just after the company's ties to homophobic organizations were revealed and their pseudo-Christian followers came out in full force. When I confronted her about it, she laid her cards on the table for the first time.

I was heartbroken. With the rest of my siblings grown and leading their own lives by the time I was four years old, Devyn was the one I'd always looked up to, the one whose approval I'd always sought. She mostly thought I was an annoying little brother (and with good reason), until I reached my teen years and became old enough for us to connect as a brother and sister who actually enjoyed each other's company.

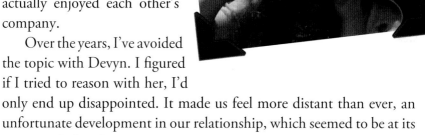

Over the years, I've avoided the topic with Devyn. I figured if I tried to reason with her, I'd only end up disappointed. It made us feel more distant than ever, an unfortunate development in our relationship, which seemed to be at its strongest before I came out.

But something changed when she had Kirby, her first child. Before he was two years old, he was diagnosed with autism. It was a learning experience for the whole family, and particularly for Devyn, who had to acclimate to raising a child with an otherness on which she had to educate herself entirely. Luckily, she had a village in her corner who was just as passionate about educating themselves on the person they love.

I think it was that same compassion that forced her to take a second look at the stigma she'd once associated with my identity. She eventually came around, just as most of the family did.

Although it's often a struggle for queer people in conservative families, some are much more fortunate. Johnny Sibilly says, "I leave that to my sister because I trust in how capable she is, even with the LGBTQ+ education I've given her. She'll call me and fill me in from time to time to make sure she's getting it right, and she always does."

My main goal as a guncle is to try to give my siblings the wisdom I'd always wished our parents had raised us with, wisdom more easily acquired as an active member of the queer community. The trick is doing it without making them feel judged, especially if you don't have experience as a parent yourself.

Nick Fager says, "Just as important as having conversations with your nieces and nephews is having convos with your siblings about gender and sexual orientation. The most powerful way to get through to your siblings about the need for open and inclusive parenting is not by lecturing on bias, but rather by vulnerably sharing your own experience with them. Maybe your father rejected your feminine traits, and you can share the pain of that with them, as well as the lasting effects. Empathy is the best conduit to change in this area."

## Guncle Wisdom

Every parent has a unique experience that cannot be fully understood by another, not unlike the nuances of queer identities. All any parent wants to do is improve upon their own parents, learning from their triumphs, as well as their mistakes.

As much as it's important to help them raise their children with a sense of social responsibility, it's just as important not to overstep or make them feel judged. If they do or say something to their kids that you want to correct, don't approach it as parenting advice (unless you're a parent yourself). Instead, relay your experience as a once-queer child and how similar parenting styles made you feel.

## *Takeaways*

- It's often the guncle's responsibility to bridge the gap between your own generation and the next.
- Don't make your siblings feel judged as parents, but offer friendly advice from the perspective of a queer former-adolescent.
- Don't underestimate their ability to expand their thinking; circle back to the tough conversations if you think the time is right.

# Chapter 8

# GUNCLE OF THE BRIDE

I was four years old the first time I attended a wedding. It was my sister Joan's, and I was quite possibly the cutest ringbearer in history, which is just an objective fact.

Granted, I kept trying to reach for the flower girl's basket as we walked down the aisle because I was jealous that she got to throw petals on the ground. But little boys were supposed to be ringbearers and little girls were supposed to be flower girls. I guess you could say I was a rebel against gender norms since the womb.

But the true torture was expecting a four-year-old to be patient enough to sit through what felt like hours of photos in every conceivable combination of all our family members. Me and my sister and her new husband. Me and both my half-sisters from my mom's side. Me and my parents. Me and my sisters and my parents. Me and my sisters and my parents and my sister's new husband and the florist (okay, that didn't actually happen). By the end of the day, I was aggravated to the verge of tears. Take that, thorough photographer!

Who would have thought that twenty-two years later I'd be the photographer at her daughter Cassie's wedding? And that experience would prove to be torture in a whole new form. Don't get me wrong, I love being my family's on-call photographer for holiday gatherings and major life events. Granted, I could probably pay off my student loans for my photography/journalism dual major by now if I'd charged for all the complimentary photo shoots I've provided for my loved ones over the years (goddess knows journalism barely pays the bills).

But this being my niece's wedding, it was a huge occasion, and I was more than happy to oblige. The conditions weren't exactly ideal for a wedding photographer, though. Most of the day was nice and relaxed, as I grabbed some shots of my niece and her bridesmaids going through hair and makeup while enjoying mimosas and finger foods.

But why my niece decided to have her wedding at a century-plus old plantation in the Deep South during the peak of summer is still a mystery to me. And why her groom-to-be's mother insisted the men in attendance wear the formal slacks and coat to the event was just insanity. Luckily, I ignored the dress code, as the building's transformer caught fire just as the guests arrived, making air conditioning in the 90-degree heat an unobtainable luxury.

I was likely drenched in sweat by the end of the day, as I was running around photographing grandparents dancing with grandchildren and bridesmaids passionately singing along to Carrie Underwood. It might not have been the most pleasant working conditions, but I managed to get plenty of great shots before the groomsmen started sweating through their rental tuxedos.

But this wasn't even the torture to which I'm referring. With three step-siblings and four half-siblings, I've reached that strange position of being the last of my generation to be unmarried with no kids. As the baby of the family, it wasn't such a big deal.

But then it skipped me and moved right on to the next generation when Cassie got engaged. Don't get me wrong, I was beyond ecstatic (not that you could gather from my resting bitch face) that she found someone who loves her and treats her well. Still, an existential crisis was pretty much inevitable.

## Guncle Wisdom

Don't compare your life to your siblings' lives, let alone your nieces and nephews' lives, especially if they're straight. It will only force you to judge yourself unfairly, taking your own accomplishments for granted.

Growing up gay, you're bound to have to come up with your own rules for your own life. Happiness doesn't mean putting a due date on major life moments. Take it at your own pace, and everything will happen at exactly the right time.

Growing up in the South, I've become accustomed to the fact that most of the people from my graduating class have tied the knot. A girlfriend I had in middle school ended up having her first child only a couple of years later. Another girl I dated for a brief moment during sophomore year has already been divorced and remarried and has had three kids with three different guys before I reached my 10-year reunion.

Things don't move quite as quickly for LGBTQ people, most of whom probably didn't grow up with a proper real-life example of the kind of life they want to lead one day. I mean, we're barely five years out from marriage equality being federally recognized, and many of us

> *Be weird. Be yourself*
> *cause at the end of the*
> *day . . . that's honestly all*
> *that matters. Let people*
> *see the real, imperfect,*
> *flawed, quirky, weird,*
> *beautiful, and magical*
> *person that you are.*
> —Colton Haynes
> (actor, model, guncle)

still see it as a patriarchal institution that would have us conform to heteronormative society.

Obviously, I'm super thrilled that same-sex marriage has become a reality in this country. But maybe it was nice having an excuse to remain single. While all my childhood friends were registering for monogrammed his & hers tongue scrapers or whatever, I could pretend I was bitter at our oppressive government and not my inability to form an emotional connection amid a series of unfortunate Grindr interactions.

Even if I was fortunate enough to have worked up the courage to come out in high school and actually maintain a stable enough relationship to result in matrimony, I was far too slutty in my early twenties to have made a marriage work so young. It's called second adolescence, the idea that most LGBTQ people, usually around their twenties, experience all the pivotal life moments and rites of passage they should have experienced in high school, when they might have been too scared to be themselves. It's actually pretty common for queer people in their young adulthood, experiencing first kisses, first loves, and all the other firsts we were deprived of during our adolescences.

Nick Fager says, "Being an out queer person means having options. You could follow the traditions that you grew up with if they align with who you are, or you could choose something completely different."

He adds, "The key is to take the time you need to get to know yourself. What makes you happy? What makes you feel satisfied? What doesn't work for you? The great gift of queerness is the ability to pave our own roads, but you want to make sure you do it in a way that aligns with who you truly are as opposed to simply rebelling against the norm or following some preconceived notion of queerness."

Growing up queer in a predominantly straightwashed environment, there's not often a rule book for how to lead a happy and healthy gay life. As if high school wasn't enough of a tragic moment, this was just another way I didn't know how to relate to my straight counterparts who mostly got married to their high school sweethearts.

Perhaps that's why I've always been able to connect so well with my nieces and nephews. We may not have had the same experiences at the same time, but I was the baby of my siblings, and I was going through my second adolescence around the time they were going through their first. If there's one thing I hope the way I live my life has taught them, it's that you can do the things you want to do on your own time without living up to some societal idea of how your life should unfold.

It was honestly no big surprise that Cassie got married before me. She always had a good blonde head on her shoulders. Even when she came to some obstacle in life, she managed to find her way over it without losing her cool. She seemed to have a plan for her life, which she stuck to with relative ease.

And she couldn't have picked a better husband. At times, I've been more than a little skeptical of people who marry their high school sweethearts, especially when it means foregoing those formative young adult years of shaping your own identity. But then I look at her parents, who got hitched right out of high school, and they're honestly the most inspiring example of a happy marriage I've had in my life.

Still, it was difficult watching my mom instantly bond with her granddaughter's new groom, just as the rest of the family had, when she never showed an interest in my love life after I came out. It makes it hard to imagine having a big happy family-filled wedding of my own when I don't even know if all my family would show up, though that mostly comes back to my own insecurities.

I remember the weekend Devyn got married in a last-minute beach ceremony on the Mississippi Gulf Coast. She'd scheduled

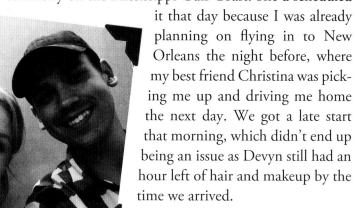

it that day because I was already planning on flying in to New Orleans the night before, where my best friend Christina was picking me up and driving me home the next day. We got a late start that morning, which didn't end up being an issue as Devyn still had an hour left of hair and makeup by the time we arrived.

Regardless, she laid into me pretty hard over the phone when she thought I'd be late, which really would have been a tragedy as I was once again the family's complimentary on-call photographer. It was a heated exchange that brought me to tears in the passenger seat of Christina's car. But I reasoned that if I suck it up to get through her wedding, they'd have to do the same for me one day, as I remained skeptical that they'd even bother attending my big gay nuptials.

Over the years, I've watched one sibling get married after another. And now, I have twenty-two nieces and nephews whose weddings I'm bound to be in attendance at before too long. As a guncle, I couldn't be prouder (if not slightly overwhelmed) at watching their lives unfold.

Meanwhile, I'm still figuring out what my life has in store.

## Guncle Wisdom

Give your family a chance every now and then, and put yourself out there, even if it's out of your comfort zone. If you're not feeling seen by those closest to you, make yourself more visible.

Coming out to a hostile environment or a family that's not 100 percent accepting can cause us to build walls and form a sense of internalized homophobia. It makes us hard to open up over time, even with our own family. But it's important to remember that people change and their thinking can evolve.

## Takeaways

- Always be there for the important life moments and show them how proud you are.
- Don't compare your life to theirs, as being queer often means forging our own unique paths.

# Chapter 9

# THE GUNCLE/FATHER

The gay uncle is probably more common than you'd think, as most families have one (whether you know it or not). But the gay father is still a rare (but growing) occurrence. I know I'm not the only one who feels a warm tingle when I scroll through Instagram to see a same-sex couple who overcame a mountain of obstacles to start their own family, a sight many hopeless queer kids probably thought they'd never see.

And although same-sex parenthood is still a rarity in most parts of the country, the benefits for their children have been proven. A 2018 study published in the *Journal of Developmental & Behavioral Pediatrics* found that children of same-sex couples are just as psychologically well-adjusted as their peers with heterosexual parents, if not more so.

Psychotherapist Nick Fager says, "Certain studies have shown that kids of openly queer parents rate higher on general health and family cohesion. It has been suggested that because queer parents do not default to gender stereotypes as much in raising their children, they are able to create a more harmonious family unit, leading to greater health and wellbeing."

He added, "I have certainly found this to be true in my work. Queer parents are generally more concerned with their kids becoming their authentic selves, rather than focusing on 'becoming a man' or 'becoming a woman.' And at the heart of so much of the wounding and trauma that I see amongst the queer population are the gendered expectations enforced on us from birth."

Regardless of whether you crave your own version of the suburban white picket fence dream or you subscribe to a more radical queer belief of rejecting the heteronormative institution of marriage, at some point or another, you've likely imagined what that Norman Rockwell kind of life looks like for you. But with limited examples of that kind of family in media or

*The one thing I'll always know is that people don't know what they want until they get it. They didn't know they wanted a song about taking a horse to the old town road in 2019. But they did.*

—Lil Nas X (musician, guncle)

even in real life, there's not often a guide or roadmap to what that looks like. Goddess knows it's not as easy for us as doing the deed on our wedding night and throwing a gender reveal party twenty weeks later.

So, whether surrogacy or adoption is your flavor, that desire to achieve a paternal sense of fulfillment is often still present. And being a guncle is usually the only experience that can prepare us for such an adventure.

Travis Heringer, a guncle and a father, told me, "Our family definitely subscribes to the village approach when raising our kids. With our nephew being the first grandkid and having a single mom, we were all hands on deck. My husband's sister is also a single mom, and he had the opportunity to be very instrumental in the raising of his nephew long before I came into the picture."

He added, "My husband and I both got the opportunity to take our guncle roles to the next level. Not only were our nephews like sons to us, but we also became father figures to them. For us, it wasn't just 'practice.' We took our role as guncles incredibly seriously and still do."

Although examples of gay fathers are few and far between, many find the duty of parenthood to transcend sexuality. As Bill Horn, father of two and guncle to Tori Spelling's kids, puts it, "I'm not sure they prepared us on how to be gay dads. But they certainly had a huge role in preparing us to be parents in general. When your two-year-old niece has a blowout and you need to change her diaper on the grass next to a busy road, one's sexual orientation doesn't seem to matter much."

My own mom and dad didn't exactly provide a roadmap for how to lead the picture-perfect family (which may not even necessarily exist). Don't get me wrong, they were great parents who gave me and my siblings the best childhoods they could, childhoods filled with fond memories. But theirs was among the 40 to 50 percent of marriages in the United States that end in divorce, and before the end, there was constant shouting that frequently drove me to the calm of the backyard, to the treehouse my uncle gave me.

Of course it was a heartbreaking experience as a child to learn of their pending divorce, as Devyn was forced to break the news to me when I hounded her with questions. But even in my annoying younger brother days, she was there to let me cry it out on her shoulder. I eventually came to appreciate their decision to end it when they did, as Gwyneth Paltrow and Chris Martin have since proven that some parents are just better off apart.

It was actually my sister Joan I often looked to as inspiration for what a family should look like. She and Luke have been married for more than twenty-five years, and they share four children who they've raised to exemplify the kind of love and acceptance I rarely saw in Mississippi. I'm sure they hit their own roadblocks along the way, but they managed to keep it together and present a strong familial front at the end of the day.

Still, it was the image of same-sex parents that I was seriously lacking throughout my impressionable years. There was my dad's friend Elliot and his husband Isaac, who had a son named Curtis. But it wasn't until I was in college that they came into my life, and theirs wasn't always the healthiest model. It was only in the last couple of years that I first felt the overwhelming vicarious joy of learning my co-worker at *OUT Magazine* was finally fostering a child with his husband after a grueling process.

Sure, there were also sporadic examples in media through such titles as *The Family Stone* and *Modern Family*, examples that have steadily become more frequent over the years. With that and the growing representation of real queer families on social media, it finally feels attainable.

I've had plenty of bonding moments with my nieces and nephews that warmed my heart, but there's one that stands out as a turning point. It happened when I was in college, and I flew to Washington State to visit my brother Ollie's family for Thanksgiving. They lived in

## Guncle Wisdom

Parenthood is a privilege often taken for granted when accidental pregnancies are about as common as fender benders and the foster system has more kids than it knows what to do with. For straight people, it's often just a natural occurrence that they've felt entitled to from an early age, when most queer kids grow up thinking a potential family of their own is unobtainable.

A bill was introduced into the Tennessee legislature in 2019 that could block LGBTQ parents from adopting on the basis of "religious freedom," a phrase often used to justify homophobia. Several other states still allow child welfare agencies to deny adopting to queer people because of similar legislation, and the surrogacy process can cost upwards of six figures in out-of-pocket expenses. Don't underestimate the dedication or ability of same-sex parents when these are often the only options they're left with.

the beautiful seaside fishing village of Anacortes, which had just been blanketed in snow.

One day when Ollie and his wife Chloe both had to be at work, I agreed to help them out by picking up my toddler twin nephews Gavin and Gabe from preschool. It was a few short blocks away, so I walked their double stroller through the pleasantly chilly suburban streets to retrieve them.

On the way back, I raced up the sidewalk and wobbled the stroller from side to side, as I could hear them giggle along the way. When we returned, it was straight to the playroom (the once-dining room filled with toys from wall to wall). All was going well until their playdate turned into hitting and pushing, a slightly more violent exchange than I was expecting from two-year-old boys. According to my brother, it was pretty normal as Gabe, the smaller twin, quickly learned how to

fight back when Gavin pushed him around.

Being the (apparently) responsible adult, I stepped in to pull them off each other, which was easy enough. It was the flood of tears that was uncontrollable.

I picked them up under each arm and sat at the base of their plastic Little Tikes slide, since no chair in that room was designed to fit my adult ass. I sat them on each knee, letting them bawl their eyes out on each shoulder. We just sat there for minutes, and I rubbed their backs until they calmed down and were ready to play again.

It was an odd sensation I'd never felt before. I didn't even know how to take care of myself yet, but I was overcome with this sense of paternal love. It was as if in that moment, my big gay version of a biological clock had begun ticking.

It was the same emotion I felt a few years later when my nephew Kirby was born, shortly before I returned home after graduating from college. He was the first of my nieces and nephews that lived close enough for me to see on a regular basis since the oldest Cassie was born.

As Devyn returned to work, she left him with our mom most days. I'd stop by her house pretty regularly on my breaks from the nearby French restaurant, where I was waiting tables while figuring out my next move. Those little daily visits established a strong bond, as this little boy unexpectedly became my best friend.

The highs also came with the lows. Kirby was often one to exhibit severe tantrums, regardless of the time or place. As it was something

Devyn dealt with frequently, I was able to approach the situation with a bit more patience, calming him down whenever I could help. But the good days always outshined the bad. If he wasn't playing around on the floor, he was fast asleep. One of the moments that consistently melted my heart was reclining all the way back in my stepdad's chair as Kirby fell asleep on my shoulder.

My friend Dan Heching, a fellow writer I've worked with on a few occasions who made the pilgrimage from New York to Los Angeles shortly before I did, had a similar experience, but with a totally different outcome. He was once tasked with babysitting his nieces and nephews. When time came to put them to bed, he picked up his baby nephew Louie, who promptly fell asleep on his shoulder.

Dan told me, "I felt the whole weight of his prone little body against me, and suddenly something clicked. I stood there and had an almost out-of-body moment, where I saw myself and simultaneously heard a voice. The voice had a very clear message, and that message was, 'This is enough.' I always had a desire to have kids, specifically to adopt a child, but as I grew up and assumed my role as an adult gay male, that particular life element began to feel like less of an immediate priority for me."

He added, "And at that moment with my nephew, I had the stark and profound realization that, not only did I no longer feel the desire to have children of my own, but I also felt imbued with a sense of well-being in the knowledge that I would be just fine without them."

For others, fatherhood is a crystal-clear goal within their grasps, regardless of the next-to-impossible hurdles that come with LGBTQ parenthood. A study conducted by the nonprofit Family Equality in 2019 found that 45 to 53 percent of LGBTQ people between the ages of 18 and 35 plan to become parents or have another child, in spite of the additional financial barriers that come with most options for same-sex parents. That's compared to 55 percent of their non-LGBTQ counterparts.

Simon Dunn said, "I've always wanted children, ever since I was a child myself. My niece and nephews have given me an opportunity to learn what it takes to be a parent, the difficulties, the benefits, and firsthand experience."

He continued, "I think deep down as gay men, we realize that having children might not happen or be an option for us. I've always been super close with my niece and nephews, so this might be a reason as to why. Mostly, I just adore them and want to be the best role model I can be and help guide them in life. There's honestly nothing greater than seeing the unconditional love they have for me; they've always been my biggest supporters along my journey."

Although I'm not entirely sure if a family is in my future, it was Devyn who recently told me she wants to see me settle down with a family of my own. That was honestly the first time someone in my family other than my nieces and nephews took that kind of interest in my future since I came out as gay. Although my mom always showed that interest in her daughters' and granddaughters' lives, I don't think she quite considered the idea of me having my own version of a family, as she'd never seen that kind of dynamic herself.

I once seriously considered getting married to a guy I fell in love with just after he got out of a fourteen-year relationship. Granted, he was thirty-seven, I was eighteen, and I still looked to Cory and Topanga in reruns of *Boy Meets World* as the ideal relationship. I didn't yet realize that gay men don't jump into monogamy with the recklessness of our straight counterparts, even after we won the long-overdue battle for marriage equality.

I've since developed a more realistic timeline for my future that's focused more on self-improvement before finding someone else who can handle my baggage. Luckily, there's plenty of babysitting and formative moments with my nieces and nephews to hold me over until I figure out exactly what I want. Being a guncle helps me build myself into the father I could potentially grow into one day.

## Guncle Wisdom

Growing up in a typical American household with a mom and dad can create some unnecessary pressure to build your own version of that family model. As queer people, we have to forge our own paths, since many of those traditions aren't tailored to us.

Regardless of what some of our heterosexual counterparts might like to believe, parenthood is not the defining moment of everyone's lives. Fulfillment comes in many forms, and the obligation to live up to a societal norm should not be one of them. If you're happy in your life without a partner or kids, let your family know. They'll come to appreciate the fact that you're the cool single guncle.

## Takeaways

- Gunclehood is the ultimate practice run for becoming a gay dad when there are so few examples in the media.
- The experience can also help you decide whether fatherhood is for you or not (either choice is perfectly acceptable).
- Since gay relationships don't always move at the same pace as their straight counterparts, don't feel pressured to make that decision too soon.

# THE INSTA GUNCLE GUIDE

The rise in popularity of the guncle is largely thanks to social media. Few can resist double tapping an adorable photo of a gay man forging a warm bond with his nieces and nephews. The hashtag "#guncle" has more than 216,000 posts on Instagram, with more being added every day. Many an Insta gay builds their brand around that unique family dynamic. We've even landed our own holiday—Guncle's Day, the second Sunday in August!

The gay influencers (or Insta gays, as they're affectionately called) of our era have made strides in pushing that representation into the mainstream.

Although I'd hardly consider myself an influencer, I've developed quite a bit of experience as a photographer. Double majoring in the field, it's ultimately taken a back seat to my work as a journalist. But I've managed to capture some quality images of gorgeous locations, historic events, and some of my favorite celebs.

I've gotten most use out of the skill with friends and family, as I'm often called on to photograph some of my loved ones' most memorable life moments. Regarded as my family's unofficial on-call photographer, I'd probably be able to pay off my student loans for that double major by now if I'd charged for half the shoots I've done back home.

From newborn announcements to senior portraits to wedding photos, I've developed quite a bit of rapport with my favorite models. And with it, I've learned a few handy tricks that every photographer should acquire for their arsenal, regardless of their skill level.

109

**Photo Tip #1**
**Lighting Is Everything**
If you can't afford a high-quality off-camera flash, you can still create a beautiful image. Natural lighting is the most valuable tool a photographer can use. You just half to know your angles and how to use them.

Direct sunlight to the face is rarely ideal for a flattering image. To reduce shadows, either wait for overcast or utilize some even shade

(trees aren't a great idea, as the light shines through leaves to cast unpredictable patterns). Backlighting is one of the easiest and most stunning effects for a quality portrait.

When photographing my niece's wedding, I made it a point to wrangle her and her groom outside right after they said, "I do." They felt obligated to greet their guests at the reception, but the sunlight waits for no one. Luckily, I got them outside and in front of the venue's fountain just as the sun was setting, creating a beautiful halo effect for a perfect photo, which ended up worth being fashionably late to the party.

**Photo Tip #2**
**Beauty in the Moment**
Although a simple selfie is often good enough to post, the beauty is in the details. Composing an aesthetically pleasing image is not hard to do if you know where to look.

Although I don't recommend straight up plagiarism, it's worth scrolling through your location's geotag on Instagram to find some photogenic spots and even some creative ideas. Wherever you are, work with the angles to achieve a unique perspective. And try to work with the elements to manipulate the composition in your favor.

While visiting my brother in Germany a couple years ago, we took a trip to Berlin over Easter weekend, where I was sure to bring my camera. I snapped some memorable moments with my niece and nephews, one of which came after jumping off at the Ostbahnhof. As another train approached the station, I told my twin nephews to hug each other and hold still while I captured them against the beautiful blurred background.

## Photo Tip #3
### Use What You Got

Just as a flash isn't necessary for a gorgeous photo shoot, neither is your own studio. Anyone can channel their inner Annie Leibovitz if they're resourceful enough.

Once again, natural light can do wonders if you have a room with a big enough window. You also don't need a backdrop if you have a minimalist wall or an aesthetically pleasing piece of fabric. And don't be afraid to get creative with simple household objects that can be used as cute props.

Shortly after one of my nephews was born, I set up a makeshift at-home photo studio at my mom's house. We stacked pillows on top of the dining room table and draped them with a blanket, all of which was right in front of a ceiling-length window. With a touch of lighting adjustments, his newborn photos came out studio quality at not even a fraction of the cost.

**Photo Tip #4**
**Color Control**

The cardinal rule of photography is that black-and-white is your best friend. Plenty of elements can go wrong with an amateur shoot, and colors are bound to clash.

This tip is most useful for those moments when the whole family manages to get together for the holidays, calling for an update on the family photo. I put it to use a few years ago during Thanksgiving, when it was a hassle just getting everyone dressed, let alone in the same color scheme. Never mind controlling the patio furniture and the neighbor's house in the background, on top of the white balance.

**Photo Tip #5**
**The Age of the Insta Guncle**

YouTube sensation Johnny Sibilly jokingly credits his massive social media success to his niece. They frequently create content together, her bubbly personality rivaling his own. In 2016, they released a comedic video entitled *When the Guncle Babysits*, which has since contributed to his more than 135,000 followers.

Travis Heringer told me, "I love seeing society starting to embrace families of all shapes and sizes. Not because it feels good for me and my husband, but because it ensures our children will grow up in a more accepting and inclusive world."

Although nieces and nephews are not just a prop to drive social media traffic, they help provide representation for different family dynamics, something that's been long overdue. And with their generation's growing reliance on social media, it never hurts to have a digitally savvy and culturally aware role model to help guide them. You don't have to be an influencer, but it's important to build a roadmap for social media responsibility for future generations to maintain.

Insta Guncle Tip #1
**Take a Back Seat**
"Make sure that it's something your niece or nephew even wants to do. Every time I fly in to see my niece, she asks, 'Can we make a video?' Or 'Did you bring your wigs?' I always love seeing gay men with their nieces and nephews, because it's a really special connection that a lot of us don't get a glimpse of."
**Johnny Sibilly**
**(@johnnysibilly)**

### Insta Guncle Tip #2
**Got to Be Real**

"Make it genuine. My favorite photos, ones I'll cherish for the rest of my life, are just of us doing what we do as a family. These include us at the beach, playing rugby, just everyday photos that record our interactions."

**Simon Dunn**
**(@bysimondunn)**

### Insta Guncle Tip #3
**Got to Be Real**

"Guncles should always be animated and ready to take over any situation to increase the fun. Be cooler than mom and dad and always have the photo filters ready, they eat that up!"

**Terrill Mitchell**
**(@tmitchell227)**

**INSTA GUNCLE TIP #4**
**Keep It PG**
"Many of us tend to use the same hashtags for all of our posts which might include some 'thirsty' tags. Make sure you edit your hashtags to be kid appropriate prior to posting."
**RJ Kennedy**
**(@rjkennedy03)**

**INSTA GUNCLE TIP #5**
**Final Approval**
"My best advice is to ask them permission to post pics. I like to let them pick pics where they think they look good. Kids are people, too!"
**Daniel Franzese**
**(@whatsupdanny)**

# Chapter 10

# THE CHOSEN GUNCLE

In case you're not yet sold on the joys of gunclehood, I assure you the guncle is one of the most under-celebrated members of any family. But not everyone is fortunate enough to have someone like that in their life. As a gay person, you'd be lucky to have that figure to look up to in the most formative years of your queer coming-of-age.

Dale Napier, an art director in Brisbane, Australia, said: "I do have a guncle myself. Growing up, while still terrified of what my family would think of me, I had some reassurance that they still spoke to and loved him (and his long-term partner whom he finally married in Australia when it became legal). So, my coming out was 'easy' thanks to the roads he had paved."

Or if you're *really* lucky, you end up like Dan Heching, who has the jackpot of guncle anecdotes: "I had a guncle who never came out to me, but whose stories and escapades have outlived him (including a brief love affair with Elton John while on a cruise in the '70s)."

*I don't in any way disparage any time I've had in the trenches because it really has made me the artist I am today.*

—Billy Porter
(actor, singer, guncle)

The closest I had was Billy, a third cousin, once removed—the only openly queer person in my distant family, other than myself. But I unfortunately never had the fortune of meeting him, as he moved to Las Vegas to become a drag queen before I was born.

My sister Joan recalls one comical memory of arriving home on the school bus sometime in the '80s to see him walking down the street in hot pants (which I can only assume was a progressive fashion choice for men in that era). Most of the extended family doesn't hold him in much high regard, justifying their disapproval with the time he dared to come home in drag one night. He's often compared to his convicted felon brother, who once locked my mom in a closet when she was babysitting them.

But one thing every queer person learns at some point or another is the importance of chosen family. When we're rejected or met with ambivalence from those who were supposedly programmed to love us unconditionally, we end up forming our own broods. Even if the family you were born into embraces you for who you are, you're likely to become an important part of someone else's chosen family.

Nick Fager says, "Try to focus on building solid relationships, and the rest will come. The curse of queerness is that it makes us default to solitude in times of distress. If you can learn to let others in, even when it is difficult, then you are on the right path. And luckily in 2020, we now have a lot of great queer role models. Find someone in your community who has found balance and satisfaction as a queer person, or someone who you can look up to in the media."

I was fortunate enough to have an older gay man in my life at the formative age of eighteen years old, when I was first com-

## Guncle Wisdom

If you have an LGBTQ child or family member who has a chosen family, it doesn't mean they love you any less or that you've failed them. It's important to remember that as a cisgender or heterosexual person, you won't be able to offer them guidance in every aspect of their lives. It often takes a village, and you could use all the help you can get. If they've found a chosen family that loves and accepts them fully, be happy for them. Make an effort to understand and appreciate that, and their chosen family could become part of your family as well.

ing to terms with my identity. His name was Elliot, and he was a close friend and former student of my dad from the early '90s. I hadn't seen him since I was five years old, but shortly after I came out to my father, he reconnected us.

Although my dad's initial reaction to my coming out was shrouded in closed-minded anger, he came around over the years. And this was one of the first acts in which I saw his thinking evolve. He knew he couldn't provide the guidance I needed in that situation, so he gave me someone who could, someone he trusted wholeheartedly. It might have felt like a simple act to him, but it meant the world to me.

It had been years since we'd last seen each other, but several memories of Elliot stood out. When I was a child we fostered his Pomeranian, Trixie, a rambunctious dog whom he loved fiercely and of whom my most prominent memory was her pooping on one of my Goosebumps books.

Another vivid memory stands out from a day when we were driving in my dad's Ford F-150, one of those single cab pickup trucks from the '80s or '90s that had no back seat. I sat in between Elliot and my dad as we left their school in Raymond. We passed a magnolia tree (the state flower of Mississippi), which I phonetically confused for mistletoe at my young age.

"Look, magnolia!" I yelled before leaning over and kissing Elliot on the mouth. He pulled away but laughed at the bizarre moment. I'm sure it was the moment he knew I was gay, if not sooner. And I didn't quite understand it then, but I always felt something kindred in him, even at that age.

When we reconnected, he quickly took me under his wing. He was a safety net, amid a sea of older gay men who wanted nothing more than to get in my pants. I'd managed to make some gay friends around my age, but they were more qualified for Smirnoff Ice-driven nights at Dick & Jane's, followed by 4:00 a.m. breakfast at Waffle House or Whataburger, where we'd watch the sun rise. Not to say those weren't important moments at that point in my life, but I also craved the wisdom of a supportive older gay man.

Elliot seemed to have the kind of life I could aspire to. He lived in a tastefully furnished house with a state-of-the-art kitchen full of gourmet ingredients for his delicious concoctions and an office full of toys and gadgets for his many hobbies. He shared it all with his husband Isaac, who worked in hospital administration and was often away on work trips, but always a joy to see. They'd been together for as long as I'd known Elliot, but I didn't quite remember meeting Isaac when I was younger.

As Elliot and I reconnected years later, I met his son Curtis for the first time. They had only recently met each other themselves, as Curtis had lived with his mom on the Mississippi Gulf Coast since he was born, and Elliot hadn't seen him since he was a baby. Given his wild anecdotes of drug-fueled exploits from his early twenties, I could see why Elliot might have decided to hold off on conquering fatherhood until a more stable point in his life.

Curtis could be described as that suburban brand of soft punk, whose iPod consisted of Green Day and Blink 182, while his closet was filled with Hot Topic labels. He was a year older than me, and we were attending the same community college at the time. Although he was straight, Curtis and I quickly connected on a level that could be described as ride-or-die, a rarity as I was quickly realizing the ignorant and judgmental nature of young straight men in the south. He was far more progressive than that.

It became so that I was quickly spending most days at their house, a place I considered a safe space and a second home. I'd even begun introducing Elliot as my uncle and Curtis as my *de facto* cousin, as it was easier than describing our complicated history and how they became the second family I so desperately needed at the time.

I think it's safe to say that they felt the same way, treating me like one of their own. They were the people I called if I needed help or if

I wanted to celebrate good news. They appreciated the kind of things my parents couldn't quite. (But I tried not to hold it against mom and dad, as one of the most useful pieces of wisdom I was given at that time was, "You've had seventeen years to come to terms with your sexuality. Give them more than seventeen minutes.")

Curtis was there to be my designated driver on my nineteenth birthday. Elliot later played DD for both of us on New Year's Eve, bringing us home to drink hot cocoa and watch the *Sex and the City* movie as the clock struck midnight, welcoming 2010. After crashing together (very platonically) in his bed, Curtis gave me a haircut in the garage the next morning, much to the disapproval of my hairstylist best friend Christina.

They were also the people to whom I introduced the guys I was dating, as my parents were nowhere near ready for that. When I introduced him to the college cheerleader Shane, it was Curtis who saw how shitty he treated me when I was only looking through hot guy goggles. With the vet tech Cal, my first sexual encounter beyond hand stuff, Isaac assured me the bumps on the back of my tongue were perfectly normal. As for the recently paroled Billy, Elliot's was the voice of reason I should have listened to for obvious reasons.

Then there was Evan, an undeniably sweet nurse, whom I got too serious with too quickly. But it was perfect while it lasted, and Elliot, Isaac, and Curtis were the family I brought him home to. Their house was a place for me and Evan to just enjoy each other's company without judgment, snuggling on the couch while watching movies and playing board games with the family. We later brought him along on our little outing to the Saint Patrick's Day parade in Jackson.

But not all chosen families last, as I would soon come to realize (to be fair, not all biological families last either).

When I went off to college in Arizona as a last resort to get away from the small minds of Mississippi, Curtis went upstate to Ole Miss.

We reconnected during winter break of our first year, when he introduced me to his new girlfriend Emily, a slightly older woman with whom he was constantly bickering. I'd spoken to her once before when she messaged me from his Facebook after reading our private messages. Elliot didn't much care for her either as she acted entitled to the monthly allowance he provided for his son.

Luckily, Curtis ended up meeting Val, a much nicer girl as Elliot told me, since I never had the pleasure of making her acquaintance myself. Before long, they were married, and I wasn't invited to the wedding. With that, Curtis suddenly stopped talking to me, never telling me why or offering closure. It was as if this new chapter of his life meant closing the book on the last.

Elliot remained in my life for a while, but things changed. When I came home from school, I made it a point to visit. But the house was empty other than him—Isaac always on work trips and Curtis settling into monogamy. It felt like Elliot had finally managed to get me to himself for some reason.

One thing led to another, and he shifted from his paternal role to something that could only be described as predatory. I wrote it off at first, as I often did with the older men who objectified me. But over time, the line was blurred, and I realized how he was taking advantage of me, manipulating and gaslighting me into going along with it. Our relationship decayed as it was suddenly poisoned with his toxic behavior.

I know. Not the uplifting story of chosen family you were expecting to hear, right? Well, it was quite the heartbreak for me too. Someone I'd considered family had used me and thrown me out like I was disposable. And with it, it felt like the innocence and hope of my youth had gone with it. His home was no longer associated with the safe space I once enjoyed, and the warm memories I did have were replaced with pain. I was abandoned.

## Guncle WIsdom

It's worth noting that in addition to the wise older gay men in my life, trans women and queer people of many identities have played a role in shaping the person I've become, as well as the LGBTQ community as a whole. But they often don't get the credit they've earned.

Chosen family transcends sexual orientation and gender identity, and it often comes in the least expected forms. Keep your heart open but strong, and you'll attract exactly the kind of people you need in your life. Just because you may have had a bad experience with your biological family doesn't mean you have to close yourself off to the love you deserve.

But don't shed any tears for me. I was young and resilient, and he was just the first of many gay men who would serve as mentors in my life. I've been fortunate enough to meet some of the wisest and most selfless queer people, many of whom have taken me under their wings over the years.

One of the first chosen guncles in my life was Lucius, someone I've actually referred to as a "dad" (not daddy, those are stories for another time). But first I should tell you about Holly.

Holly was a bartender at Dick & Jane's when I first started frequenting the establishment. She was always studying for med school behind the bar (she's now a talented kickass entrepreneur in New Orleans). In addition to the great conversation she frequently provided, she offered some pretty decent guidance. At one point, I began jokingly referring to her as my mother. It stuck over the years, and she'll refer to me as her son as well.

When I told her about my dreams of moving to New York City, she connected me with one of her oldest friends. She and Lucius were best friends since their days at Rutgers in the early '90s. Although our correspondence was mostly through Facebook for a while, I also began jokingly referring to Lucius as my "dad."

It was Lucius who helped me get my first summer internship in the city, connecting me to his friend Brian, who worked in human resources at Christie's Auction House. It set off a chain reaction, which helped me line up internships at *OUT Magazine* and *Teen Vogue* for the following summers. To this day, I credit Holly, Lucius, and Brian with jumpstarting my career.

In addition to his career guidance, Lucius also offered me my first couch to crash on when I arrived in Manhattan. He introduced me to the gay bars and kink shops of Christopher Street and 8th Avenue, and with it, the rich and vibrant queer community of Chelsea and the West Village that spanned generations.

He also invited me into the weekly tradition of Sunday brunch with the boys at The Dish. "The boys" consisted of the aforementioned Brian, who would offer a couch for me the next summer, Ray, the drag queen who lived in the basement apartment below Lucius, and Ray's brother Daryl, a graphic designer who always carried a journal full of sketches and his daily haikus. If Lucius was a second father of sorts, they would become my chosen guncles.

They were frequently nearby for two-for-one happy hour drinks at Gym Bar or a glass of wine at Le Grainne, the French café on the corner of 21st and 9th, two doors down from Lucius' apartment. It was a cozy little spot, frequented by our neighbors Ethan Hawke and Faye Dunaway.

Although nobody can agree on who it was, one of them taught me the "look-back." It's a trick from the ancient gay art of cruising, which was how queer people found casual sex long before the days of dating apps and gay bars as bachelorette party venues. The "look-back" (which I've also referred to as the "three-second-rule") involves walking past a hot guy on the sidewalk, waiting three seconds and looking back. If he looks back too, he's interested. It actually worked once when my phone broke, and I couldn't get on Grindr.

The boys were also there for my twenty-first birthday, an evening that started innocently enough with my first (legal) drink at the historic Stonewall Inn. It then carried up to Hell's Kitchen, where we barhopped with a cute boy with whom I was having a summer fling. The night ended with a late dinner that almost happened at the now-shuttered 24-hour

> *I don't care whether people like me or dislike me. I'm not on earth to win a popularity contest. I'm here to be the best human being I possibly can be.*
>
> **—Tab Hunter (actor, guncle)**

New Venus Diner, where I ended up puking on the sidewalk outside before my food even came to the table. Luckily, Lucius was there to put me in a cab home (and to make sure I remembered where home was).

Over the years, Holly, Lucius, and I would have sporadic family reunions in New York or New Orleans. If it was only two of us, we'd raise a glass to the other, who was always on our minds. The same went for the rest of the brunch boys whenever we were in the same city.

By the time I finished college and was ready to move to New York full-time, Brian had moved to Los Angeles. Shortly after, Lucius relocated to the Big Easy, where he was closer to mom. Ray and Daryl were still around, but I didn't see them quite as much as when we had our standing brunch dates.

Although nobody could replace them, I soon expanded my chosen family. During my early days as a freelancer at *OUT*, I found a side gig as a waiter and barback at Barracuda, a gay bar that served as a Chelsea staple and a filming location for a scene from *Sex and the City* (if the name RickNinePlus rings a bell, you know what scene I'm referring to). It was one of those charming little hidden-away spots that hosted queer locals and tourists alike, with nightly performances by *RuPaul's Drag Race* contestants-to-be.

The new side hustle also came with a group of happy hour regulars I quickly took to. Their near-daily patronage turned out to be more dependable than the L train service to Brooklyn. And it was a dependability that began to feel familial in a city where nobody knew their neighbor.

Michael was a fellow writer and bon vivant of sorts, who was married to Edmund White, one of my favorite authors who once belonged to the seminal Violet Quill. There was also Joe, a gay preacher, who had no issue participating in the often-inappropriate banter that ensued during a slow happy hour. Josh was the bartender I worked with most days, a sober tatted playful spirit who always kept the laughs coming.

Their company was a refreshing dose of queer community, a contrast from the late-night crowd, which was usually a bevy of hot guys with their faces glued to their phone screens. Slow days were more enjoyable when they were around, calling their unofficial salon to order over half-price cocktails. Although I was only at that job for less than a year before picking up more writing work, they left a mark I still fondly reminisce about.

It doesn't take a supportive family or a stable home life to make a good guncle. We come in all forms, and we're there when you need us most. Fairy godmothers may not be real, but we're the next best thing.

## *Takeaways*

- Chosen family is often a crucial part of the queer experience, especially if your biological family rejects you.
- Having a chosen family doesn't mean they're replacing your biological family, but it is important to have people in your life who understand your struggles.

# RESOURCES

**AIDS Healthcare Foundation (AHF)**
The AIDS Healthcare Foundation provides HIV prevention services, testing, and healthcare for HIV patients around the world. Find more information online at AIDSHealth.org.

**Ali Forney Center**
Based in New York City, this is the largest LGBTQ community center, aimed at providing homeless youth with transitional housing. Find more information online at AliForneyCenter.org.

**Free Mom Hugs**
This group of parents and allies aims to educate families, church members, and civic leaders on the LGBTQ community. They also provide temporary financial assistance for a variety of support, and they'll even stand in for your parents at your same-sex wedding if needed. Find more information online at FreeMomHugs.org.

**Human Rights Campaign (HRC)**
The largest LGBTQ civil rights organization in the country, the Human Rights Campaign advocates for equality and educates the public on issues facing our community while fighting for LGBTQ-inclusive policies. Find more information online at HRC.org.

**Lambda Legal**
The Lambda Legal Defense and Education Fund advocates for civil rights of LGBTQ people and those living with HIV, providing legal

support through impact litigation, education, and public policy work Find more information online at LambdaLegal.org.

### Lighthouse App
This New York City-based app is steadily expanding nationwide to connect users with LGBTQ-affirming healthcare professionals, including founder Nick Fager's bicoastal Expansive Therapy. Find more information online at Lighthouse.LGBT and ExpansiveTherapy.com.

### Parents and Friends of Lesbians and Gays (PFLAG)
Parents and Friends of Lesbians and Gays unites the LGBTQ community with families and allies, accessible at more than 400 chapters across the United States. Find more information online at PFLAG.org.

### Planned Parenthood
In addition to providing lifesaving reproductive healthcare globally, Planned Parenthood is the largest provider of sex education in the nation, with LGBTQ-focused resources being just one part of their broad range of programming. Find more information online at PlannedParenthood.org.

### The Trevor Project
This suicide hotline offers safe and confidential support from trained counselors for LGBTQ youth. They can be reached at their 24-hour toll-free number, 1-866-488-7386, or online at TheTrevorProject.org.

# BIBLIOGRAPHY

Morton, M.H., Dworsky, A., & Samuels, G.M. (2017). Missed opportunities: Youth homelessness in America. National estimates. Chicago, IL: Chapin Hall at the University of Chicago.

CDC. (2016). Sexual Identity, Sex of Sexual Contacts, and Health-Risk Behaviors Among Students in Grades 9-12: Youth Risk Behavior Surveillance. Atlanta, GA: U.S. Department of Health and Human Services.

The Trevor Project. (2019). National Survey on LGBTQ Mental Health. New York, New York: The Trevor Project.

Baiocco, Roberto, Nicola Carone, Salvatore Ioverno, and Vittorio Lingiardi. "Same-Sex and Different-Sex Parent Families in Italy." Journal of Developmental & Behavioral Pediatrics 39, no. 7 (2018): 555–63. https://doi.org/10.1097/dbp.0000000000000583.

Family Equality (2019) LGBTQ Family Building Survey. https://www.familyequality.org/fbs

# ACKNOWLEDGMENTS

I cannot begin to express the proper gratitude for my family, who's always managed to be there for me, regardless of whether or not we see eye-to-eye. Writing so honestly about our family was often difficult, and I know it couldn't have been too easy for you, so thank you for being patient with me. I literally couldn't have done it without you.

To my high school English teachers Lisa May and Mary Porter, thank you for nurturing my passion for writing from an early age.

And to Aaron Hicklin, I'm eternally grateful that you took a chance on me as an intern back in the day. My career and successes are thanks to you.

Thank you to Nick Fager, psychotherapist, LMHC, LPCC, founder of Expansive Therapy, and the beautiful mind behind @gaytherapy on Instagram. You're an amazing therapist and an even better friend. You've always been there for me, and this book would not be possible without you.

To my chosen family Holly Williams, Lucius Riley, Brian McComak, Ray Richardson, Daryl Richardson, Mark Murphy, Craig Dolezel, Anthony Colantone, Seth Nickerson, Christina Nievas, Marcus Martin, Christian Aguilar, and Morgan Winsor, I'm lucky to have found you. You make it a very happy life.

Thanks also to Daniel Franzese, Johnny Sibilly, RJ Kennedy, Francesco "Franco" DeMarco, Dan Heching, Simon Dunn, Bill Horn, Dale Napier, Travis Heringer, R Kurt Osenlund, Terrill Mitchell, and Blake P. for trusting me with sharing your experiences.

# ABOUT THE AUTHOR

Glenn Garner is a Mississippi boy by birth but princess of Genovia at heart. He grew up in Jackson with a profound love for movies and a wild sense of imagination that would take him far beyond the closed-minded views of the south.

After attending Terry High School, he made the leap to Flagstaff, Arizona, sheerly for the opportunity to get out and expand his horizons. There, he dual-majored in photography and journalism at Northern Arizona University. It was also there that he came into his identity as a queer person, penning the school newspaper's first LGBTQ column "So Over the Rainbow" and serving on the board of the school's gay-straight alliance, People Respecting Individuals and Sexual Minorities (PRISM).

Following college and several misguided career moves back home in Jackson, he moved to New York City, where he worked for nearly five years at *OUT Magazine*, the country's most circulated LGBTQ publication. Working his way up to editor, he interviewed the likes of Boy George, Lily Tomlin, and several *RuPaul's Drag Race* queens, also covering events like New York Fashion Week, Art Basel, and the inaugural Women's March on Washington, DC.

Glenn currently resides in Los Angeles, California, where he can enjoy a more relaxed yet always fun lifestyle, as well as the joys of legalized marijuana. He currently freelances for several publications and media outlets, always looking to expand his cultural and creative experiences.